Jacob Kaminsky

THERE IS A GOD!?

Copyright © Jacob Kaminsky

The right of Jacob Kaminsky to be identified as author of this work has been asserted by him in accordance with section 77 and 78 of the Copyright, Designs and Patents Act 1988.

All rights reserved. No part of this publication may be reproduced, stored in a retrieval system, or transmitted in any form or by any means, electronic, mechanical, photocopying, recording, or otherwise, without the prior permission of the publishers.

Any person who commits any unauthorized act in relation to this publication may be liable to criminal prosecution and civil claims for damages.

A CIP catalogue record for this title is available from the British Library.

ISBN 978 184963 758 9

www.austinmacauley.com

First Published (2014)
Austin Macauley Publishers Ltd.
25 Canada Square
Canary Wharf
London
E14 5LB

Printed and bound in Great Britain

Foreword

This book was written mainly as a search for the god Jehovah (also rendered as Yahweh, YHWH) and its origins. But along the way I came across various scenarios which I thought proper to include as an introduction to this book. Among the scenarios are such that drove me to this research. Most I saw fit to record in their chronological order, more or less.

My interest in Jehovah began even before I turned seven. At the time, I was in my second year of *Talmud Torah* (Jewish school focusing on Hebrew and Bible studies) in the neighborhood where I grew up. My parents were hard-up, hard-working religious folks. I shall never forget that day. After school, on my way home, I ran into a group of somewhat older kids, maybe two to three years older, who – like so many other kids worldwide – began to pick on me, maybe on account of the French-style blue beret I was wearing … Within a split second one boy jumped at me, grabbed the beret off my head and ran away, and the other kids all followed him. At that moment my heart sank, I began sobbing, covered my head with my hands, and ran home, keeping my hands on my head.

"What happened?" asked my father, but I was so upset I couldn't even reply. "What's wrong with your head? Move your hands away, let me see," my father kept saying, but I wouldn't answer or take my hands off my head. Only after my father pried one of my hands off my head did I tell him, all chocked up with tears, that my beret had been stolen.

"That's all?" asked my dad. "I thought you'd been hurt," he said, trying to remove my hands from my head, while I fought him with all my might, screaming:

"The Divine Presence will escape! It will leave me!"

"Trust me, son, it won't escape. You can remove your hands from your head ..." Gradually, his soothing words sank in, and my father got me to take my hands away from my head.

That day was a turning point in my life. I refused to go back to *Talmud Torah*; I had lost my pure, innocent faith in God; and I stopped sleeping with a beret on.

Though I lost my pure faith, I continued paying attention to the difference between truth and lies, and was of two minds when it came to belief in Jehovah; I truly wanted to belong to the band of believers. I recall how, years later, at a point of crisis in my life, I tried to find religion again, become a born-again Jew. One of my colleagues at work got to me, and helped me on my way back to religion. I began changing my life style and at the same time to extricate myself from the crisis. As it happens, I got over the crisis, gave up on returning to religion for the time being and carried on with my life.

After completing my compulsory IDF service, I went back to the job I had before being drafted, and after work hours I studied various subjects – my favorite occupation all my life. Initially, I went to night school, but never managed to complete a course, because I kept being interrupted by call-ups for Reserve Duty. I finally decided to change the way I studied and became an autodidact, concentrating on whatever interested me at the time, be it physics, chemistry, math and languages.

While studying physics and chemistry, one of my favorites soon became the Russian chemist Dmitri Ivanovich Mendeleyev, born in 1834 in Tobolsk, Siberia, died in 1907 in St Petersburg. The youngest among his siblings, orphaned at a young age and having suffered poverty and hardships, he nonetheless made it to St Petersburg university where he studied physics, math and mainly chemistry. His great achievement, as is well known today, is the Periodic Table. I was immensely impressed by the fact that his method enabled us to learn about the existence and properties of elements that had not yet, in practice, been discovered; and by the fact that he was the first person to record in a clear, organized manner all elements and materials from which God created the heavens and the earth. He listed the elements in his table according to their atomic weight and valence, and arranged the elements by categories. I felt that Mendeleyev could easily have taken his list of elements to the Vatican, say, and claimed that God dictated to him the precise list of ingredients from which he created the universe, and become a saint ... All the more so since nowhere in the Bible does it say what materials God used to make the world. But I suppose Mendeleyev's integrity prevented him from taking that route, and he remained a highly respected Russian scientist.

Another figure who caught my fancy was prolific American-Jewish writer Sholem Asch. Born in Poland in 1880, he spent most of his life in the United States, but later emigrated to Israel where he spent the last couple of years of his life. He wrote mostly in Yiddish, and his works were translated into several languages. One day I read in the paper that Asch, a religious Jew, was kicked out of a synagogue where he went to pray on the Sabbath. The reason given was his novel *The Nazarene*, which – so it was claimed – was 'missionary', preaching conversion to Christianity. I had not read anything by Asch at that point, but found it difficult to comprehend how a Jew could have been thrown out of synagogue; and not just any Jew, but one that had earned international acclaim! I'd never heard of such a case before, and got very curious. Why had he been driven away? What did he write that provoked such a reaction? I inquired among my friends – especially the religious among them – whether they'd heard of the case, and did they think it right to expel a fellow Jew from synagogue. All were unanimous in their replies, that the expulsion was totally justified! That made me all the more curious, and I wished to know – what was it that he had written? Guess what – none of my friends had read the book! I had no choice but to go out and buy it. Along with several others by Asch. Naturally, I began with *The Nazarene*.

I found the novel to be a literary gem. To this day I consider it one of the best books I've ever read. I found nothing in it offensive to the Jewish religion (in my opinion, at least,) and needless to say it did not sway me religiously – I neither became a Christian nor changed my beliefs in any way.

Regardless of Sholem Asch, I'm all for rational writing that is meant to enlighten, educate, and even try to influence a person's views; the more a person keeps an open mind and reads, the better. But it should be kept in mind that some people deliberately spread disinformation in order to prevent the truth from reaching those who seek it. Back to Asch: Since that case at the synagogue, dozens of years ago, I have not yet met a single person who has read *The Nazarene*, neither in Israel nor in any of the other numerous countries I've visited … I gather, then, that his novel did Judaism no harm at all, and driving Asch out of synagogue was totally superfluous and pointless.

The revered writer was not the only person to be treated shamefully by synagogue officials. One day I was invited to synagogue on a Saturday, on the occasion of a friend's son's bar mitzvah, where the boy was going to read his portion of the Torah. I must have been a bit late, because everyone was already seated and praying. This synagogue was set up inside an apartment, where the wall separating two rooms had been removed. It was a Reform synagogue, which was a new thing to me. Until then I had no idea that Judaism, like other religions, had different 'streams', and each had its own customs. I myself had been brought up in a traditional Orthodox Jewish home.

At the entrance to the synagogue I was greeted by the local wheeler-dealer who handed me a folded prayer shawl. I didn't know anyone there; as a rule, I don't attend synagogue, except when invited to a special occasion, like this one. I found a free spot and sat down. The prayer shawl I'd been given was filthy and stank of stale perspiration and mold. I put it on the bench beside me. The wheeler-dealer who gave me the prayer shawl saw, and indicated that I should put it on. Had it been clean, I would have wrapped myself in it as is the custom without being told. I motioned to him that the prayer shawl was right here beside me and all was well. But he kept insisting, in motions, that I put it on. Since I didn't want to make a noise or cause a commotion in the midst of the service, I simply ignored him, assuming he'd leave me alone. But he made his way over to me, and insisted I leave the place, ostensibly because my behavior was desecrating the holy place. Without saying a word, I got up and walked out, missing the ceremony. I waited outside for my wife, who was in the women's section, which is out of bounds for men. When the service was over, a woman – probably a pillar of the community – came over to me and asked what had happened. I told her, stressing how filthy and smelly the prayer shawl was. Since I come from a very religious background, I keep my personal prayer shawl, which I got for my bar mitzvah, in perfect condition, beautifully clean, ironed and folded, in my wardrobe.

"You're right," said the woman, "but we have no budget for laundry." I thought the answer was ridiculously unsatisfactory. Either don't use prayer shawls if you can't afford to keep them clean, or else make an effort and hand-wash them once in a while, if wearing them means so much to you.

Last year I took my vacation at the Club Med in Sicily. As usual at those clubs, the food is good, the beach clean, the water in sea and pool clear and inviting. At night there are shows and entertainment, followed by dancing until the wee hours. You can join various fun activities, partake in sports on a competitive or non-competitive basis, and go on tours. I joined one such tour of a typical Sicilian town. On the bus there, I asked our guide what we were going to see there, to which he only answered in Italian:

"*Sorpresa!*" i.e., surprise. The bus stopped right outside an ancient looking church that was, like the many other churches I'd seen, exceedingly beautiful. Inside, looking at the ceiling, I immediately recognized the painting: it depicted Pontius Pilate washing his hands in a basin, with an inscription of the phrase attributed to him.

"I am innocent of the blood of this person". Feeling a bit uncomfortable, I followed my urge and asked the guide:

"Tell me please, where was Jesus from? What was his nationality?"

"Italiano!" the guy responded with great conviction.

"But how can this be? Didn't all this take place in Jerusalem?"

"Yes!"

"So how did such an important person get from Italy to Jerusalem?"

The guide was obviously surprised by my question. Since he seemed an educated person, I pursued the matter:

"Could you please find out for me? It means a lot to me."

"With pleasure."

"See you tomorrow in the dining room?"

"Sure!"

The following morning, as I was having my breakfast, when the guide passed by my table, I asked him:

"Well, have you found out for me?"

"Yes! He was Italiano!" he replied just as convinced as before, and trotted off, looking upset and angry.

That was the last I saw of him.

At this point I'd like to discuss a movie I saw – Mel Gibson's *The Passion of the Christ* – depicting the last hours of Jesus's life, before the crucifixion.

This film portrays the Romans of the time (whom we'd refer to as Italians today) as a cruel, sadistic people. When the Roman soldiers viciously flagellate Jesus, the Jews who were – according to the movie – among the crowd at the beginning of the whipping, were sick at the sight and left, while the Romans as depicted by Gibson continued on merrily. The Roman people at the time had the strongest empire in the world. Pontius Pilate, the administrator ('Prefect') of Judea on behalf of the Roman Empire, was known for his cruelty, and was even called back to Rome and chided for his excessive cruelty. This same Pontius, later declared as a saint by the Christian church, sentenced Jesus to death without a trial. The Jewish people who purportedly took part in the whipping are the same people who suffered starvation under the corrupt rule of the family of the Roman-appointed Jewish high priest. As is well known, Jesus himself was a Jew; his claims that he was the

Son of God, or the Messiah, appear only in Christian sources. The Jews, from ancient times to this very day, yearned for the coming of the Messiah, and many who lived in the times of Jesus apparently believed that he indeed was the Messiah. The Jews, therefore, must have been the last ones to want the Jewish Jesus dead. And he indeed died a Jew.

The movie very clearly promotes Christian beliefs, even at the expense of Judaism. Even if the film did provoke a brief spell of anti-Semitism by awakening a dormant hatred in some, I believe that on the whole the movie has done a cruel disservice to Christianity. On the one hand, the movie portrays Jesus as claiming to be God's son or messenger, yet neither son nor Father can save him from his awful predicament. I'd say that's a serious shortcoming of both! Jesus is shown as totally helpless. And this begs the most important question asked since Jehovah created the world: Have you ever known a father who would not help his son in his hour of need? And at such a major crisis in his life? When such horrible trouble befalls his beloved only son? When this father is not just any father, but Our Father Who Art in Heaven, the great creator of the universe, the greatest god ever? Why, this movie casts irrevocable aspersions at God and at Christianity alike!

To my eyes, this film looks like a commercial for whips and nails more than anything else ... An interesting piece of trivia is that the nails made for this movie in time for its screening were sold for $17 per nail and were quickly sold out. Quite a record for nail sales ... Another fact worth mentioning is that the wife of the bloody killer Pontius Pilate was also recognized as a saint by the Christian Church.

Christianity evolved from a certain Jewish Messianic sect, one of several that were in existence at the time. A bunch of people from that sect followed Jesus, seeing in him the Jewish Messiah. Jesus himself was Jewish and remained so until his dying day. He lived in Nazareth and had many admirers in that town and its environs; clearly he was no ordinary man. Jesus was a highly religious person who preached adherence to Jewish values, and was probably tantamount to what today would be a venerable rabbi. One day he decides to get up and go to Jerusalem together with his faithful flock. What was it that could entice a respectable, God-fearing Nazarene man to leave everything behind and go to Jerusalem? Keep in mind that Jesus would have had to walk all the way from Nazareth to Jerusalem, some hundred miles, risking highway robbers, wild animals, and who knows what other perils. Remember, too, that Jesus and his followers were poor people, who lived sparsely. Well then, I ask, what was the attraction? Oh yes: it was the Temple, the House of God.

In those days, the Temple in Jerusalem, considered to be the House of God, attracted Jews from near and far who made the pilgrimage in order to pray to God and make sacrifices to him. The sacrifices included cattle and sheep, fowl, wheat and oil, and more. Of course, much of these could not be carried from afar, and had to be purchased relatively nearby. It is all too likely that the courts around the Temple were lined with market stalls, probably belonging to the family of the high priest, who ruled the country with an iron fist. Now imagine Jesus, the respected preacher, arriving with his pupils and followers at this center of corruption. Picture him getting on a soapbox and beginning to preach, talking of honesty, fairness, adhering to the values of Judaism, and not turning the house of the Lord into a marketplace. Who knows, maybe he even knocked over a few market stalls in his attempt to make his point. Naturally, many flocked to listen and to join him. I believe it is unlikely that the Jews, who loved Jesus and respected him and his war against corruption, would try to get him killed.

These events, as well as his ongoing campaign against corruption, were not in his favor when the owner of the stalls heard about them. From here to the bribe received by Pontius Pilate, the way to the basin and water and the "I am innocent of the blood of this person" plea, the path was short. As we know, today too, wherever someone tries to fight corruption, he may gain the covert respect and sympathy of those around him, but no more; most will clam up, not wanting to put themselves in harm's way; since the strong and the corrupt are those who call the shots.

In those days, the early first century CE, the situation in Judea was very bad. The country was governed by the despotic Pontius Pilate as representative of the Roman Empire, and the high priest Hanan, who with his two sons and under the auspices of Pilate, ruled Jerusalem. As often happens among oppressed people, here too messianic movements developed that strived for a dramatic change. Such movements usually form around charismatic people, and they set their sights high: liberation from foreign oppressors or tyranny, and yearning for thorough social and/or political change. Such movements arose before and after Jesus; he was neither the first nor the last, whether in olden-times Judea or in modern day countries to this very day. The crisis brought about by Herod assuming power and Rome's oppression of Judea were the catalysts for the emergence of new leaders and new messianic ideas; Jesus was but one of the Jews at the time – albeit the most famous one – who claimed they were the saviors of their people, and paid for it with their lives. In that sense it was indeed a tragic period of brave and short-lived freedom-fighters and self-proclaimed saviors.

And if we're talking of saviors and messiahs, this is the place to introduce Joan of Arc – Jeanne d'Arc, the young peasant girl who lived in France in the fifteenth century and, claiming that she had visions from God, led the French army in the fight against the English. The Church condemned her as a heretic and a witch, and sentenced her to death by burning. The Inquisition gave Jeanne d'Arc the option of retracting her claim that she had a divine revelation in which case she would be pardoned. But she refused, preferring to be burnt at the stake. Years later, a retrial reversed her conviction and she was proclaimed as St Joan of Arc, a saint of the Roman Catholic Church. Could it be that the Church had already known the truth full well at the time?

Moving forward to modern times: One day I went with a group of volunteers on a trip to Jerusalem to see an art exhibition of works by international glass sculptor Dale Chihuly. The exhibition took place at a breathtaking location – the Tower of David in the Old City of Jerusalem, a beautifully conserved ancient citadel, which made a perfect setting for Chihuly's art. It was nearly midnight by the time we left, and raining lightly, but our guide, a native Jerusalemite, offered to take us on a tour on foot, including the ultra-orthodox neighborhood Meah Shearim. Our group consisted of people in their sixties and seventies; but being warmly dressed and equipped with umbrellas, we set out. I clearly remember it was a Thursday, because we stopped by a bakery that was already selling freshly baked challah for the Sabbath.

We reached an open square among the houses of Meah She'arim, where we stood around our guide who in a low voice began his explanation. Curious about the place, I moved a few steps away from the group and looked around. One of the apartment houses, nicknamed the Hungarians' House, had a long balcony with an iron railing, and was brightly lit. A man came out onto the balcony on the second floor, and I couldn't take my eyes off him: good-looking, with a long, flowing white beard, he looked like the Messiah the way I pictured him in my childhood ... Suddenly the man pointed at our group and started hollering in Yiddish – a language I'm fluent in, since it is my mother-tongue:

"Pour water on them! Pour water on them!"

Before I could recover from my surprise, a strong young man of twenty or so, in Orthodox garb with the ends of his prayer shawl sticking out, growled at me:

"Get out of here! Clear out, I'm telling you, immediately!" and started pushing me. I was aghast. The physical and vocal assault made me feel as if I were on the brink of a pogrom. I'd been pushed around in the past, in my youth, by hostile Arabs. But here? At my age? In my own country? Among religious Jews, who are supposed to be of superior morality? However, I quickly rallied round, and forcing my voice to sound loud and masterful I bellowed back at him:

"Thou shalt not kill!" and somehow my words brought the would-be thug back to reality. The "messiah" figure went back indoors and the thug left, as if nothing happened. We walked back to the bus that awaited us and drove back home.

My foreword would not be complete if I don't let you in on my following revelation:

[26] Then God said, "Let Us make man in Our image, according to Our likeness; let them have dominion over the fish of the sea, over the birds of the air, and over the cattle, over all[b] the earth and over every creeping thing that creeps on the earth." [27] So God created man in His own image; in the image of God He created him; male and female He created them. (Genesis 1, 26-27.)

These verses make it clear that Man looks exactly like God. Nowhere in Scriptures is there an exact description of the humans created by God. In addition, God is usually conceived of as invisible but all-seeing. Well, in that case, the humans He created must also be like The Invisible Man! Yet, according to well-established archeological findings, it has been proven that prehistoric man lived on Earth scores of thousands of years ago, around 150,000 years ago. For those who doubt it, I wish to remind them of the dinosaurs and their ilk, who also lived here on planet Earth hundreds of thousands of years ago, and are not mentioned at all in Scriptures. Those prehistoric men, who look more-or-less like modern man and they are indeed the same creature. Moreover, according to Judaism and all Torah thinkers of all ages, the world was created by God only 5771 years ago ... Whereas we, descendents of prehistoric man, have been around far longer ... It therefore follows that the creatures created by God less than six thousand years ago and named by Him, Adam and Eve (Or rather, Adam and Hava, since English wasn't quite the Lingua Franca yet), are definitely not one and the same as the creatures (you and I) who walk the Earth today. So we can assume that Invisible Man is alive and well somewhere amongst us. As we know, their ancestors ate from the Fruit of Knowledge, while, judging by the evidence, most visible people on earth have not. So it seems possible that there are two types of Adam and Eve living on Earth at present.

If that's the case, the question is when, why and how did Homo Sapiens overrun his divine counterpart and usurp his identity. I sure hope that the divine man-creature, being highly intelligent and created in the image of God and ate the fruit of the Tree of Knowledge, isn't just passively hiding as he watches Homo Sapiens destroy Earth.

Now in my later years, as I sit in my Health Services' clinic waiting room, there's a religious Jew complete with beard and sideburns sitting opposite me and arguing with a few others sitting there waiting for their appointment. The topic of their discussion is yeshiva students, in principle exempt from compulsory military service, while some in government wish to get them to enlist and serve in the IDF. It isn't my habit to interfere in conversations of people I know, all the more so when it comes to strangers. But, having listened so far and found the man's arguments irrational, I could no longer restrain myself from butting in. I asked,

- What about one of the most important commandments, which comes before 'Thou shalt not kill', namely, '8 Remember the Sabbath day, to keep it holy. 9 Six days you shall labor and do all your work, 10 but the seventh day is the Sabbath …' (Exodus 20:8-10)

- "What does the word labor, or work, mean to you?" He countered.

- "For me it means to create, produce, build, make something!"

- "Well, for me the word work means cock-a-doodle-doo! Anyone can interpret the written word any way he wishes!"

Well, that was news to me … I had no idea what to say to that, so I said nothing and moved away. I was angry with myself for not being able even to try a retort to his false logic, despite all the years I'd invested in studies. I had always wanted to read the Pentateuch (the Five Books of Moses) closely, but always left it for 'later'. But this chance encounter made me want to search for the truth, and where would that be found, if not in the Torah? So the very next morning I began to explore the book of Genesis. I did it methodically and thoroughly, writing down each verse where I found a mistake, or where the written word did not sit well with rational reality. I carried on systematically, writing down my comments while doing my best to extract the truth out of the events described. I must say that more than once I changed my views and beliefs throughout my research.

Note: Unless stated otherwise, all bible quotations are from the New King James version.

Genesis

'And God said' -- these words appear many times in the creation story, but said to whom? That is an important question! Since all his words were written down, who was doing the writing? After all, God had yet to create man.

1:24-31

[24] Then God said, "Let the earth bring forth the living creature according to its kind: cattle and creeping thing and beast of the earth, each according to its kind"; and it was so. [25] And God made the beast of the earth according to its kind, cattle according to its kind, and everything that creeps on the earth according to its kind. And God saw that it was good.

[26] Then God said, "Let Us make man in Our image, according to Our likeness; let them have dominion over the fish of the sea, over the birds of the air, and over the cattle, over all the earth and over every creeping thing that creeps on the earth." [27] **So God created man in His own image; in the image of God He created him; male and female He created them.** [28] Then God blessed them, and God said to them, "Be fruitful and multiply; fill the earth and subdue it; have dominion over the fish of the sea, over the birds of the air, and over every living thing that moves on the earth."

[29] And God said, "See, I have given you every herb that yields seed which is on the face of all the earth, and every tree whose fruit yields seed; to you it shall be for food. [30] Also, to every beast of the earth, to every bird of the air, and to everything that creeps on the earth, in which there is life, I have given every green herb for food"; and it was so. [31] Then God saw everything that He had made, and indeed it was very good. So the evening and the morning were the **sixth day**.

God created man and woman on the sixth day of creation. God created man <u>in Our image, according to Our likeness</u> (1:26), the word "our" obviously referring to God himself and others like him (since in Hebrew there is no honorific 'we' that refers to a single person). It seems God belonged to a particular group of beings that all looked alike.

2:8-9

[8] The Lord God planted a garden eastward in Eden, and there He put the man whom He had formed. [9] And out of the ground the Lord God made every tree grow that is pleasant to the sight and good for food. The tree of life was also in the midst of the garden, and the tree of the knowledge of good and evil.

God puts man in the Garden of Eden, without a mate.

2:18-20

[18] And the Lord God said, "It is not good that man should be alone; I will make him a helper comparable to him." [19] Out of the ground the Lord God formed every beast of the field and every bird of the air, and brought them to Adam to see what he would call them. And whatever Adam called each living creature, that was its name. [20] So Adam gave names to all cattle, to the birds of the air, and to every beast of the field. But for Adam there was not found a helper comparable to him.

And we see that man still has no mate!

2:21

[21] And the Lord God caused a deep sleep to fall on Adam, and he slept; and He took one of his ribs, and closed up the flesh in its place.

God does not create woman simply by saying so, as he created the world and all that is in it, but sets about the task of creating woman by hand, which is why she is the most beautiful part of creation. Finally, after a difficult delivery, man officially has a mate. Why have I lingered on these sentences which tell us that God created woman on the sixth day and then that it is not good that the man should be alone, and finally that man has a mate on the eighth day of creation? Because from the very beginning of the Bible it is clear that the writer paid no attention to small important details. Based on the beginning of Genesis it is apparent that God is not the one writing the book or else it would have started "In the beginning I created the heaven and the earth ..."

The Bible is generally accepted as The Book of Books, the ultimate book. It has examples of every kind of literature: beautiful poetry, profound serious philosophy, proverbs and fables with exceptional morals, very interesting stories, a collection of important laws to allow humans to live together in harmony, and finally a record of ancient history. All these written in rich, beautiful Hebrew.

Obviously the Bible was not written by one person, it was written by many people over generations. The men who wrote the Bible were smart, educated people - each in comparison to the general knowledge of his time. One cannot ignore that the Bible contains children's stories at an incredible literary level. Let me further explain that last statement by directing the reader to books such as Saint-Exupery's *The Little Prince*, Coelho's *The Alchemist* (not strictly a children's book, though the protagonist is a boy), De Luca's *God's Mountain*, and the greatest of all, J.K. Rowling's Harry Potter books, in which many readers find deeply meaningful philosophy though they were written for children and teenagers. Authors wrote books for children in ancient times as well, and the best of them were deemed suitable by the compiler of the Bible to be included in it, where appropriate. Some of the prominent children's stories in the Bible are the creation story, Noah's Ark, and the biggest story of all - Exodus. In any case, the creation story, as a tale, is a very nice tale. But it would be unfair of me not to comment on the fact that all animals and all birds, without exception, no matter how primitive, know exactly what to do in their life. That is, how to reproduce, how to take care of their young, when to feed them and take care of them, when to let them go to live their own lives in nature, and all this without a bite from the tree of knowledge. In contrast, man, who is supposedly the smartest animal of all, needs to live at least a quarter of its life before he shows interest in reproducing, and after all that, he has no clue how to raise his children and prepare them for life - despite having eaten from the tree of knowledge.

2:10-15

[10] Now a river went out of Eden to water the garden, and from there it parted and became four riverheads. [11] The name of the first is Pishon; it is the one which skirts the whole land of Havilah, where there is gold. [12] And the gold of that land is good. Bdellium and the onyx stone are there. [13] The name of the second river is Gihon; it is the one which goes around the whole land of Cush. [14] The name of the third river is Hiddekel [Tigris]; it is the one which goes toward the east of Assyria. The fourth river is the Euphrates.
[15] Then the Lord God took the man and put him in the garden of Eden to tend and keep it.

Therefore, the Garden of Eden is located north of the Persian Gulf, in Kuwait along the border with Iran, where the Tigris and the Euphrates flow into the sea, after they converge north of the city Basra in Iraq. This is the only place where the two rivers meet, and from there they flow as one river into the Persian Gulf. The Euphrates and the Tigris (Hiddekel) both originate in the mountains of Turkey, but from locations that are very far apart.

2:10

[10] Now a river went out of Eden to water the garden, and from there it parted and became four riverheads.

The author of this story did not know of the geographical concept that all streams flow into the sea and so thought that all streams flow from the sea to land especially when a huge delta is created where the river flows into the sea and so sometimes one can see water flowing to the sea or the land (i.e. tide).

4:3-5

[3] And in the process of time it came to pass that Cain brought an offering of the fruit of the ground to the Lord. [4] Abel also brought of the firstborn of his flock and of their fat. And the Lord respected Abel and his offering, [5] but He did not respect Cain and his offering. And Cain was very angry, and his countenance fell ... and it came to pass, when they were in the field, that Cain rose up against Abel his brother and killed him.

To begin the first story of man's life on Planet Earth with a murder, and to put the blame on God for not accepting Cain's offering, therefore pushing Cain to kill his brother Abel, does hurt the sanctity of the book, and of course is a rather big blow to God himself. The tradition of offering a sacrifice to God originates in an ancient pagan custom that was in practice long before the Bible (that is 5,769 years ago). The sacrifices were mostly humans whose flesh was eaten immediately after the ceremony. Over generations when the savage tribes evolved towards humanism the nature of the sacrifice changed from man to beast, whose flesh was also eaten immediately after the ceremony. These feasts were not necessarily conducted in public, but after the ceremony, and were attended only by those who served the holy deity and their families. Among the

Israelites this custom continued until the destruction of the Second Temple.

4:13-14

[13] And Cain said to the Lord, "My punishment is greater than I can bear! [14] Surely You have driven me out this day from the face of the ground; I shall be hidden from Your face; I shall be a fugitive and a vagabond on the earth, and it will happen that anyone who finds me will kill me."

4:17

[17] And Cain knew his wife, and she conceived and bore Enoch. And he built a city, and called the name of the city after the name of his son—Enoch.

Cain was the son of Adam and Eve, who were the only people in the whole world! So it is not quite clear who could claim Cain's life and kill him. Not only that, but now suddenly he has a wife. And with regards to the city — did he build the city on his own? For whom? And most importantly, if he did not build it himself, where did he find workers and who were these workers?

6:2

[2] that the sons of God saw the daughters of men, that they were beautiful; and they took wives for themselves of all whom they chose.

This verse confirms what I mentioned above, that God belonged to a group of beings that all looked like him, and here he already had children and they took wives from among the humans – which shows that humans did indeed resemble God in looks.

6:5-8

⁵ Then the Lord saw that the wickedness of man was great in the earth, and that every intent of the thoughts of his heart was only evil continually. ⁶ And the Lord was sorry that He had made man on the earth, and He was grieved in His heart. ⁷ So the Lord said, "I will destroy man whom I have created from the face of the earth, both man and beast, creeping thing and birds of the air, for I am sorry that I have made them." ⁸ But Noah found grace in the eyes of the Lord.

God regrets creating man and decides to annihilate the entire human race and all his creation and make a new world.

8:21

²¹ And the Lord smelled a soothing aroma. Then the Lord said in His heart, "I will never again curse the ground for man's sake, although the imagination of man's heart is evil from his youth; nor will I again destroy every living thing as I have done.

It turns out that there was another man on the Ark, and, of course, it was he who wrote down everything that happened. This was a man of exceptional talent to be able to read the mind of God.

As far as we know, marriage among relatives may result in children who suffer from mental retardation. If we follow the first man on the face of the planet we will realize that his descendants all suffered from some mental retardation. There were also wicked men who could not tell the difference between good and evil, despite the fact that their parents ate from the tree of knowledge. So evil were they that God decided to wipe all living creatures off the face of the earth, including the human race — except for Noah who was a righteous man! He was charged with building the Ark and preserving what little good remained on the earth in the Ark, including his own family. Let us not forget that in the ark there were eight people plus the writer of the story, all cooped up together with the animals, the livestock, the birds and creeping things of the earth, all of course evacuating their bowels in the Ark. The smell and fumes should have killed all living creatures aboard the closed Ark in less than a week, even if it was well ventilated — which it wasn't. And despite this, they survived. After the world was cleansed for a hundred and fifty days, Noah and his family emerged into a new, clean, well-washed world to receive God's blessing "multiply and fill the earth". Now, what do you think about marriage among relatives?

Another point that cannot be ignored is that no specimen from among the dinosaurs was brought onto the Ark, since, at the time, dinosaurs no longer existed on the planet. This proves that the world was created long before the date set by the Jewish faith. Dinosaur fossils have been found for centuries. In the 17th century they were first identified as belonging to an unknown species, and in the 19th century the first dinosaur species were identified in England and the term itself was coined. Since then, skeletons and bones of many kinds of dinosaurs have been discovered all over the world. In China skeletons have been found of a number dinosaur species that lived about a million years ago.

6:18-20

[18] But I will establish My covenant with you; and you shall go into the ark—you, your sons, your wife, and your sons' wives with you. [19] And of every living thing of all flesh you shall bring two of every sort into the ark, to keep them alive with you; they shall be male and female. [20] Of the birds after their kind, of animals after their kind, and of every creeping thing of the earth after its kind, two of every kind will come to you to keep them alive.

9:8-11

[8] Then God spoke to Noah and to his sons with him, saying: [9] "And as for Me, behold, I establish My covenant with

you and with your descendants after you, [10] and with every living creature that is with you: the birds, the cattle, and every beast of the earth with you, of all that go out of the ark, every beast of the earth. [11] Thus I establish My covenant with you ...

The first person to have a serious, real, though one-sided, conversation with God is Noah. Until now we did not read about any covenant between God and Noah and his family.

12:1-2

Now the Lord had said to Abram: "Get out of your country, from your family and from your father's house, to a land that I will show you [2] I will make you a great nation; I will bless you and make your name great; and you shall be a blessing.

12:5

[5] Then Abram took Sarai his wife and Lot his brother's son, and all their possessions that they had gathered, and the people whom they had acquired in Haran, and they departed to go to the land of Canaan. So they came to the land of Canaan.

12:7

[7] Then the Lord appeared to Abram and said, "To your descendants I will give this land." And there he built an altar to the Lord, who had appeared to him.

Abram was the second person to truly see God. Abram developed a strong relationship with God who tells him to leave the house of his father and go to an unknown land where God promises to make Abram into a great nation. Abram made his way by foot with all of his property, family and attendants. In those days there were no hotels, inns or restaurants so the whole entourage spent their nights outdoors, in the open. Food they actually had aplenty; Abram would slaughter a sheep or lamb according to the number of diners. At the time there was no electric stove or portable kitchen, so they had to be built, generally of stones that could be found in the open. This custom is very efficient, though it developed from an older pagan custom, when the food was usually human flesh. There were always ways to convince someone that it was his turn to be eaten — and these methods are still used today! I know of at least one recent instance that took place in the U.S., and while all Americans know of this incident, they do not see the correlation — so I will tell you of it. A man arrives in the US from a foreign country, enrolls in flight lessons in some flight school where he learns how to pilot large planes; he then hijacks such a plane and crashes it into a skyscraper in New York. Of course that was no simple feat, this man was no ignoramus with low intelligence, but an educated man, and yet he was convinced it was his time to be eaten. A trend is developing in the world today, there are more and more people whose job it is to convince other people to wear explosive belts and blow themselves up in crowded places. But let's return to the topic of building altars. The god I believe in does not need sacrifices, he also does not particularly enjoy the smell of roasting meat. I suspect altogether that he's a vegetarian! But I know that the people working at the altar do love a good roast. The mere roasting of meat on a device made of stones outdoors can be seen as a religious ceremony.

12:6-8

[6] Abram passed through the land to the place of Shechem, as far as the terebinth tree of Moreh. And the Canaanites were then in the land.

[7] Then the Lord appeared to Abram and said, "To your descendants I will give this land." And there he built an altar to the Lord, who had appeared to him. [8] And he moved from there to the mountain east of Bethel, and he pitched his tent with Bethel on the west and Ai on the east; there he built an altar to the Lord and called on the name of the Lord.

We witness the strong relationship between Abram and God. Once again we see the building of the altar for God. One could interpret this simply as building a device for cooking roasts and pita, which is the bread that the inhabitants of this region eat to this day. Or one could possibly see these altars as a device for roasting meat in order to please the gods.

12:11-16

[11] And it came to pass, when he was close to entering Egypt, that he said to Sarai his wife, "Indeed I know that you are a woman of beautiful countenance. [12] Therefore it will happen, when the Egyptians see you, that they will say, 'This is his wife'; and they will kill me, but they will let you live. [13] Please say you are my sister, that it may be well with me for your sake, and that I may live because of you."

[14] So it was, when Abram came into Egypt, that the Egyptians saw the woman, that she was very beautiful. [15] The princes of Pharaoh also saw her and commended her to Pharaoh. And the woman was taken to Pharaoh's house. [16] He treated Abram well for her sake. He had sheep, oxen, male donkeys, male and female servants, female donkeys, and camels.

This incident made me very angry! How could Abram, who had such a close relationship with God, and who always remembered to build an altar whenever he relocated and call on the name of the Lord, at this critical moment forget his God? One gets the impression that he does not believe in God at all, or perhaps this was because it had to do with his wife. At the time a woman was of no importance, so Abram might not even bother to waste a penny on her, despite having won much property. To this day women are considered property in much of the Middle East.

13:1-4

Then Abram went up from Egypt, he and his wife and all that he had, and Lot with him, to the South. ² Abram was very rich in livestock, in silver, and in gold. ³ And he went on his journey from the South as far as Bethel, to the place where his tent had been at the beginning, between Bethel and Ai,⁴ to the place of the altar which he had made there at first. And there Abram called on the name of the Lord.

The lack of reference to Sarai, Abram's wife, in this story shows how little women were valued in those times. But Abram is portrayed as a real man - a winner! After leaving Egypt with great fortune Abram remembers his God and goes back to an old camp where he had built an Altar and calls on the name of the Lord.

13:14-17

¹⁴ And the Lord said to Abram, after Lot had separated from him: "Lift your eyes now and look from the place where you are—northward, southward, eastward, and westward; ¹⁵ for all the land which you see I give to you and your descendants forever. ¹⁶ And I will make your descendants as the dust of the earth; so that if a man could number the dust of the earth, then your descendants also could be numbered. ¹⁷ Arise, walk in the land through its length and its width, for I give it to you."

14:17-20

¹⁷ And the king of Sodom went out to meet him at the Valley of Shaveh (that is, the King's Valley), after his return from the defeat of Chedorlaomer and the kings who were with him.
¹⁸ Then Melchizedek, king of Salem, brought out bread and wine; he was the priest of God Most High.¹⁹ And he blessed him and said: "Blessed be Abram of God most high,

possessor of heaven and earth; [20] And blessed be God most high, who has delivered your enemies into your hand." And he gave him a tithe of all.

17:8

[8] "Also I give to you and your descendants after you the land in which you are a stranger, all the land of Canaan, as an everlasting possession; and I will be their God."

These verses clearly show that God gave the land of Israel to all of Abram's descendants – both Ishmael and Isaac who were his sons -- it is God's will! We as the people of Israel must share this land with the Arabs who are the descendants of Ishmael, Abram's eldest son.
The wars that the Jewish people wage against the Arabs go against God's will. But this promise changes in the future at Sarah's request, who is the wife of Abraham.

15:1-6

[1] After these things the word of the Lord came to Abram in a vision, saying, "Do not be afraid, Abram. I am your shield, your exceedingly great reward."
[2] But Abram said, "Lord God, what will You give me, seeing I go childless, and the heir of my house is Eliezer of Damascus?" [3] Then Abram said, "Look, You have given me no offspring; indeed one born in my house is my heir!"
[4] And behold, the word of the Lord came to him, saying, "This one shall not be your heir, but one who will come from your own body shall be your heir."[5] Then He brought him outside and said, "Look now toward heaven, and count the stars if you are able to number them." And He said to him, "So shall your descendants be."
[6] And he believed in the Lord, and He accounted it to him for righteousness.

15:7-13

⁷ Then He said to him, "I am the Lord, who brought you out of Ur of the Chaldeans, to give you this land to inherit it."
⁸ And he said, "Lord God, how shall I know that I will inherit it?"
⁹ So He said to him, "Bring Me a three-year-old heifer, a three-year-old female goat, a three-year-old ram, a turtledove, and a young pigeon." ¹⁰ Then he brought all these to Him and cut them in two, down the middle, and placed each piece opposite the other; but he did not cut the birds in two. ¹¹ And when the vultures came down on the carcasses, Abram drove them away.
¹² Now when the sun was going down, a deep sleep fell upon Abram; and behold, horror and great darkness fell upon him. ¹³ Then He said to Abram: "Know certainly that your descendants will be strangers in a land that is not theirs, and will serve them, and they will afflict them four hundred years.

Abram starts to doubt God's promises, even though God is with him in the tent and they are having a serious business-like conversation. As proof of his word, God performs a pagan ceremony filled with magic and sorcery. But any connection between this ceremony and Abram's doubts is hard to come by. This is, by the by, the first bit of sorcery mentioned in the Bible, which is supposedly performed by God. The mere penning of this story and its connection to God is blasphemy! Or perhaps Abram was merely hallucinating.

17:1-8

¹ When Abram was ninety-nine years old, the Lord appeared to Abram and said to him, "I am Almighty God; walk before Me and be blameless. ² And I will make My covenant between Me and you, and will multiply you exceedingly." ³ Then Abram fell on his face, and God talked with him, saying: ⁴ "As for Me, behold, My covenant is with you, and you shall be a father of many nations. ⁵ No longer shall your name be

called Abram, but your name shall be Abraham; for I have made you a father of many nations. ⁶ I will make you exceedingly fruitful; and I will make nations of you, and kings shall come from you. ⁷ And I will establish My covenant between Me and you and your descendants after you in their generations, for an everlasting covenant, to be God to you and your descendants after you. ⁸ Also I give to you and your descendants after you the land in which you are a stranger, all the land of Canaan, as an everlasting possession; and I will be their God."

17:9-12

⁹ And God said to Abraham: "As for you, you shall keep My covenant, you and your descendants after you throughout their generation... Every male child among you shall be circumcised; ¹¹ and you shall be circumcised in the flesh of your foreskins, and it shall be a sign of the covenant between Me and you.¹² He who is eight days old among you shall be circumcised, every male child in your generations ...

17:14

¹⁴ And the uncircumcised male child, who is not circumcised in the flesh of his foreskin, that person shall be cut off from his people; he has broken My covenant."

God was hurt by creating man in his image, so now he makes a covenant with Abram, after renaming him Abraham, and orders him to remove the foreskin of every male child when he is eight days old. This covenant helped maintain the Jewish people a small people, that has gotten even smaller over the years. I will not bother searching through the whole history of the Jewish people, but I cannot ignore the Holocaust, when this covenant helped the Germans find Jews and burn them in concentration camps!

As a true believer in God, who knows that everything that happens is God's will, I cannot understand why he chose to reduce the number of Jews in the world, or even wipe them out completely. It started with the flood and has gone on for generations. In contrast, those who did not follow God's statute and did not remove the foreskin, he has spared their lives and strengthened their countries and people.

17:17

[17] Then Abraham fell on his face and laughed, and said in his heart, "Shall a child be born to a man who is one hundred years old? And shall Sarah, who is ninety years old, bear a child?"

18:11

[11] Now Abraham and Sarah were old, well advanced in age; and Sarah had passed the age of childbearing.

20:2-4

[2] Now Abraham said of Sarah his wife, "She is my sister." And Abimelech king of Gerar sent and took Sarah.
[3] But God came to Abimelech in a dream by night, and said to him, "Indeed you are a dead man because of the woman whom you have taken, for she is a man's wife."
[4] But Abimelech had not come near her ...

20:14-18

[14] Then Abimelech took sheep, oxen, and male and female servants, and gave them to Abraham; and he restored Sarah his wife to him. [15] And Abimelech said, "See, my land is before you; dwell where it pleases you." [16] Then to Sarah he said, "Behold, I have given your brother a thousand pieces of silver; indeed this vindicates you before all who are with you and before everybody." Thus she was rebuked.

[17] So Abraham prayed to God; and God healed Abimelech, his wife, and his female servants. Then they bore children; [18] for the Lord had closed up all the wombs of the house of Abimelech because of Sarah, Abraham's wife.

The story of Sodom and Gomorrah dwarfs in comparison to these stories. Again I ask, where is Abraham's faith in God? But there is another issue, just such an incident had already taken place with Pharaoh, the King of Egypt (Genesis 12:11). In Egypt Abraham came out of the whole ordeal with great wealth, as he did again, but back then Sarah was young and beautiful, now she is ninety years old! I don't see why the writer chose to repeat this story. Perhaps this is plagiarism, and having liked the first story the writer put it in again, though it makes no sense here. What is interesting, is that all the women in the royal family of Abimelech King of Gerar could not conceive, and only after Abraham prayed to God (this time he does pray to God) did all the ladies' wombs open within such a short time! Even the best hospitals and fertility clinics in the country can't produce test results so quickly, though thousands of years have passed and they have all the newest technologies and labs. The important question is: How did all the women in King Abimelech's family know, within a day, that their wombs had closed? We must not forget that they were as primitive as can be. Gershwin said it best in one of his song – 'It Ain't Necessarily So'.

Through the repetition of the incident that happened with Pharaoh, which was odd in and of itself, we understand that the writer thought he was exulting the name of God, though it is this repetition that actually harms God. Again, I get the impression that Abraham tended to hallucinate.

18:7-8

[7] And Abraham ran to the herd, took a tender and good calf, gave it to a young man, and he hastened to prepare it. [8] So he took butter and milk and the calf which he had prepared,

and set it before them; and he stood by them under the tree as they ate.

These verses describe the three angels' visit to Abraham's home, who came to his wife Sarah to give her the news of the birth of her son Isaac in the near future. There is nothing odd about the men of God eating meat and milk and butter all in one meal! The meal was prepared according to Abraham's request, who at this point in time, was the only man to ever have a one-on-one conversation with God. Incidentally, the Bible never states that one should separate meat and dairy. The whole issue of eating meat and dairy separately is based on the verse 'You shall not boil a young goat in its mother's milk' (Exodus 23:19), which appears in two other places in the Bible and simply states that you must not boil a young goat in its mother's milk! The language is simple, it needs no explanation or interpretation. I should add here that one must not, under any circumstance, explain or interpret the words of God, and those who do so, without exception, debase God and put themselves above him and they will be punished accordingly!

26:3-5

[3] "Dwell in this land, and I will be with you and bless you; for to you and your descendants I give all these lands, and I will perform the oath which I swore to Abraham your father. [4] And I will make your descendants multiply as the stars of heaven; I will give to your descendants all these lands; and in your seed all the nations of the earth shall be blessed; [5] because Abraham obeyed My voice and kept My charge, My commandments, My statutes, and My laws."

Until now we never saw what precepts, laws and statutes (apart from circumcision) God and Abraham had agreed upon, so the above verses are completely irrelevant at this point. But again, these may be just more of those hallucinations that afflict Abraham from time to time.

21:9-13

⁹ And Sarah saw the son of Hagar the Egyptian, whom she had borne to Abraham, scoffing.¹⁰ Therefore she said to Abraham, "Cast out this bondwoman and her son; for the son of this bondwoman shall not be heir with my son, namely with Isaac." ¹¹ And the matter was very displeasing in Abraham's sight because of his son.

¹² But God said to Abraham, "Do not let it be displeasing in your sight because of the lad or because of your bondwoman. Whatever Sarah has said to you, listen to her voice; for in Isaac your seed shall be called. ¹³ Yet I will also make a nation of the son of the bondwoman, because he is your seed."

Due to Sarah's anger at her bondwoman Hagar, God improves on his promise to Abraham and disinherits Ishmael, son of Hagar, from inheriting the land, promising instead that he will be compensated with another land. God indeed compensated Ishmael with many other lands: Jordan, Syria, Lebanon, Egypt, Saudi Arabia, Iraq, Iran, Yemen, Sudan, Libya, Algeria, Tunisia, Morocco, Afghanistan etc. Clearly God compensated Ishmael very generously.

26:6-9

⁶ So Isaac dwelt in Gerar. ⁷ And the men of the place asked about his wife. And he said, "She is my sister"; for he was afraid to say, "She is my wife,"because he thought, "lest the men of the place kill me for Rebekah, because she is beautiful to behold."⁸ Now it came to pass, when he had been there a long time, that Abimelech king of the Philistines looked through a window, and saw, and there was Isaac, showing endearment to Rebekah his wife.⁹ Then Abimelech called Isaac and said, "Quite obviously she is your wife; so how could you say, 'She is my sister'?"

This is the third time that a similar story appears in Genesis. Twice with Abraham as the protagonist, who seems to have suffered from hallucinations and delusions, but here Isaac plays the main role.

11:31

[31] And Terah took his son Abram and his grandson Lot, the son of Haran, and his daughter-in-law Sarai, his son Abram's wife, and they went out with them from Ur of the Chaldeans to go to the land of Canaan; and they came to Haran and dwelt there. [32] So the days of Terah were two hundred and five years, and Terah died in Haran.

12:1-3

[1] Now the Lord had said to Abram: "Get out of your country, from your family and from your father's house, to a land that I will show you. [2] I will make you a great nation; I will bless you and make your name great; and you shall be a blessing. **3** I will bless those who bless you, and I will curse him who curses you; and in you all the families of the earth shall be blessed."

12:7

[7] Then the Lord appeared to Abram and said, "To your descendants I will give this land."

13:14-15

[14] And the Lord said to Abram, after Lot had separated from him: "Lift your eyes now and look from the place where you are—northward, southward, eastward, and westward; [15] for all the land which you see I give to you and your descendants[b] forever.

14:14-16

14 Now when Abram heard that his brother was taken captive, he armed his three hundred and eighteen trained servants who were born in his own house, and went in pursuit as far as Dan. **15** He divided his forces against them by night, and he and his servants attacked them and pursued them as far as Hobah, which is north of Damascus. **16** So he brought back all the goods, and also brought back his brother Lot and his goods, as well as the women and the people.

15:1

After these things the word of the Lord came to Abram in a vision, saying, "Do not be afraid, Abram. I am your shield, your exceedingly great reward."

15:18

18 On the same day the Lord made a covenant with Abram, saying:
"To your descendants I have given this land,

15:7

7 Then He said to him, "I am the Lord, who brought you out of Ur of the Chaldeans, to give you this land to inherit it."

20:6

6 And God said to him in a dream, "Yes, I know that you did this in the integrity of your heart. For I also withheld you from sinning against Me; therefore I did not let you touch her. **7** Now therefore, restore the man's wife; for he is a prophet, and he will pray for you and you shall live.
(the dream of Abimelech king of Gerar)

21:22-23

²² And it came to pass at that time that Abimelech and Phichol, the commander of his army, spoke to Abraham, saying, "God is with you in all that you do. ²³ Now therefore, swear to me by God that you will not deal falsely with me, with my offspring, or with my posterity; but that according to the kindness that I have done to you, you will do to me and to the land in which you have dwelt."

22:1-2

¹ Now it came to pass after these things that God tested Abraham, and said to him, "Abraham!"
And he said, "Here I am."
² Then He said, "Take now your son, your only son Isaac, whom you love, and go to the land of Moriah, and offer him there as a burnt offering on one of the mountains of which I shall tell you."

22:10-12

¹⁰ And Abraham stretched out his hand and took the knife to slay his son.
¹¹ But the Angel of the Lord called to him from heaven and said, "Abraham, Abraham!"
So he said, "Here I am."
¹² And He said, "Do not lay your hand on the lad, or do anything to him; for now I know that you fear God, since you have not withheld your son, your only son, from Me."

In previous chapters we witness that God forces his presence on Abraham and catches him in all sorts of of situations – outdoors, in his tent, in a vision and in his dreams, and promises to Abraham over and over again the land of Israel, in different sizes and with different borders, including the people who lived in those lands. Abraham goes to do battle against the kings who took captive Lot (his brother's son), his family, and his property. For this purpose he gathers three hundred and eighteen men from his servants, chases after and catches up with these kings. He then subdues the kings, frees Lot along with his family and property and returns them to their home. Of course, returning from such a victory he gains much respect among the kings he defeated. Among the kings who come to greet him is:

14:18-20

[18] Then Melchizedek king of Salem brought out bread and wine; he was the priest of God Most High. [19] And he blessed him and said: "Blessed be Abram of God most high, possessor of heaven and earth; [20] And blessed be God most high, who has delivered your enemies into your hand."

In fact, Abraham receives the highest honours for the period and place where he lived. But Abraham was convinced he deserved more; he wanted land and to be a king like all the kings around him. They even courted his company, which he rightly deserved as he was strong, rich, and wise. His life continues peacefully until one day Abraham received a message from God which orders him to:

22:2

[2] "Take now your son, your only son Isaac, whom you love, and go to the land of Moriah, and offer him there as a burnt offering on one of the mountains of which I shall tell you."

And this is where I am suddenly alerted and ask, why would God require this? And I start thinking and remember that when Abraham went down to Egypt he was afraid that Pharaoh would take Sarai his wife, despite all of God's promises, despite God's protection. And again Abraham feared King Abimelech who was his friend, even though Sarah was already ninety years old. It becomes clear that all of God's unreasonable demands are simply these hallucinations that come over Abraham from time to time. Even after the incident of sacrificing his son Isaac, Abraham continues in his delusions.

22:15-18

[15] Then the Angel of the Lord called to Abraham a second time out of heaven, [16] and said: "By Myself I have sworn," says the Lord, "because you have done this thing, and have not withheld your son, your only son— [17] blessing I will bless you, and multiplying I will multiply your descendants as the stars of the heaven and as the sand which is on the seashore; and your descendants shall possess the gate of their enemies. [18] In your seed all the nations of the earth shall be blessed, because you have obeyed My voice."

26:1-11

[1] There was a famine in the land, besides the first famine that was in the days of Abraham. And Isaac went to Abimelech king of the Philistines, in Gerar.
 [2] Then the Lord appeared to him and said: "Do not go down to Egypt; live in the land of which I shall tell you. [3] Dwell in this land, and I will be with you and bless you; for to you and your descendants I give all these lands, and I will perform the oath which I swore to Abraham your father. [4] And I will make your descendants multiply as the stars of heaven; I will give to your descendants all these lands; and in your seed all the nations of the earth shall be blessed; [5] because Abraham obeyed My voice and kept My charge, My commandments, My statutes, and My laws."
 [6] So Isaac dwelt in Gerar. [7] And the men of the place asked about his wife. And he said, "She is my sister"; for he was afraid to say, "She is my wife," because he thought, "lest the men of the place kill me for Rebekah, because she is beautiful to behold." [8] Now it came to pass, when he had been there a long time, that Abimelech king of the Philistines looked

through a window, and saw, and there was Isaac, showing endearment to Rebekah his wife. ⁹ Then Abimelech called Isaac and said, "Quite obviously she is your wife; so how could you say, 'She is my sister'?"

Isaac said to him, "Because I said, 'Lest I die on account of her.'"

¹⁰ And Abimelech said, "What is this you have done to us? One of the people might soon have lain with your wife, and you would have brought guilt on us."¹¹ So Abimelech charged all his people, saying, "He who touches this man or his wife shall surely be put to death."

The man who chronicled the story of Abraham's life must have been his best friend, for Abraham confessed to him all of his thoughts and dreams, his visons, his expectations of God, his hallucinations and his fear that various kings would take away his wife Sarah. After Abraham's death the writer no longer had any juicy stories to write, so he decides to write of Isaac. Obviously starting on chapter 26, the first thing he writes is a summary of the life of Abraham father of Isaac, to link them together as he begins telling Isaac's chronicles. Later he saw he had enough material to work with, even without writing about God, so he abandoned that direction, but not before he wrote the following verse:

26:24

²⁴ And the Lord appeared to him the same night and said, "I am the God of your father Abraham; do not fear, for I am with you. I will bless you and multiply your descendants for My servant Abraham's sake."

It is evident that God did not develop a relationship with Isaac, Abraham's son, but he later renews his relationship with Abraham's descendants through Jacob:

28:10-16

[10] Now Jacob went out from Beersheba and went toward Haran. [11] So he came to a certain place and stayed there all night, because the sun had set. And he took one of the stones of that place and put it at his head, and he lay down in that place to sleep. [12] Then he dreamed, and behold, a ladder was set up on the earth, and its top reached to heaven; and there the angels of God were ascending and descending on it.

[13] And behold, the Lord stood above it and said: "I am the Lord God of Abraham your father and the God of Isaac; the land on which you lie I will give to you and your descendants. [14] Also your descendants shall be as the dust of the earth; you shall spread abroad to the west and the east, to the north and the south; and in you and in your seed all the families of the earth shall be blessed. [15] Behold, I am with you and will keep you wherever you go, and will bring you back to this land; for I will not leave you until I have done what I have spoken to you."

[16] Then Jacob awoke from his sleep and said, "Surely the Lord is in this place, and I did not know it."

28:20-22

[20] Then Jacob made a vow, saying, "If God will be with me, and keep me in this way that I am going, and give me bread to eat and clothing to put on, [21] so that I come back to my father's house in peace, then the Lord shall be my God. [22] And this stone which I have set as a pillar shall be God's house, and of all that You give me I will surely give a tenth to You."

31:3

[3] Then the Lord said to Jacob, "Return to the land of your fathers and to your family, and I will be with you."

31:10-19

[10] "And it happened, at the time when the flocks conceived, that I lifted my eyes and saw in a dream, and behold, the rams which leaped upon the flocks were streaked, speckled, and grey-spotted. [11] Then the Angel of God spoke to me in a dream, saying, 'Jacob.' And I said, 'Here I am.' [12] And He said, 'Lift your eyes now and see, all the rams which leap on the flocks are streaked, speckled, and grey-spotted; for I have seen all that Laban is doing to you. [13] I am the God of Bethel, where you anointed the pillar and where you made a vow to Me. Now arise, get out of this land, and return to the land of your family.'"

[14] Then Rachel and Leah answered and said to him, "Is there still any portion or inheritance for us in our father's house? [15] Are we not considered strangers by him? For he has sold us, and also completely consumed our money. [16] For all these riches which God has taken from our father are really ours and our children's; now then, whatever God has said to you, do it."

[17] Then Jacob rose and set his sons and his wives on camels. [18] And he carried away all his livestock and all his possessions which he had gained, his acquired livestock which he had gained in Padan Aram, to go to his father Isaac in the land of Canaan. [19] Now Laban had gone to shear his sheep, and Rachel had stolen the household idols that were her father's.

31:24

[24] But God had come to Laban the Syrian in a dream by night, and said to him, "Be careful that you speak to Jacob neither good nor bad."

31:29

[29] It is in my power to do you harm, but the God of your father spoke to me last night, saying, "Be careful that you speak to Jacob neither good nor bad."

Rachel and Leah are mad at their father, since he had sold them and all their money, and they tell Jacob to follow God's wishes. Rachel herself did not believe in the God Jehovah, and so, just in case, stole her father's household idols.

After the many years Laban spent in Jacob's company, Laban became a believer in the God of Jacob, and at times even dreams of him and receives orders. However, he still chases after Jacob when he sees his idols missing. When he catches up he searches carefully for the idols, but they are still in Rachel's possession who hid them under her camel's saddle. As she was in 'the manner of women' her father did not ask her to get off the camel.

32:9

⁹ Then Jacob said, "O God of my father Abraham and God of my father Isaac, the Lord who said to me, 'Return to your country and to your family, and I will deal well with you'

32:24-29

²⁴ Then Jacob was left alone; and a Man wrestled with him until the breaking of day. ²⁵ Now when He saw that He did not prevail against him, He touched the socket of his hip; and the socket of Jacob's hip was out of joint as He wrestled with him. ²⁶ And He said, "Let Me go, for the day breaks."

But he said, "I will not let You go unless You bless me!"

²⁷ So He said to him, "What is your name?"

He said, "Jacob."

²⁸ And He said, "Your name shall no longer be called Jacob, but Israel; for you have struggled with God and with men, and have prevailed."

²⁹ Then Jacob asked, saying, "Tell me Your name, I pray."

And He said, "Why is it that you ask about My name?" And He blessed him there.

32:30

[30] So Jacob called the name of the place Peniel: [Literally Face of God] "For I have seen God face to face, and my life is preserved."

35:1-4

[1] Then God said to Jacob, "Arise, go up to Bethel and dwell there; and make an altar there to God, who appeared to you when you fled from the face of Esau your brother." [2] And Jacob said to his household and to all who were with him, "Put away the foreign gods that are among you, purify yourselves, and change your garments. [3] Then let us arise and go up to Bethel; and I will make an altar there to God, who answered me in the day of my distress and has been with me in the way which I have gone." [4] So they gave Jacob all the foreign gods which were in their hands, and the earrings which were in their ears; and Jacob hid them under the terebinth tree which was by Shechem.

Jacob decides to remove all the foreign gods from his household and among his companions and chooses the Lord as his god.

35:9-13

[9] Then God appeared to Jacob again, when he came from Padan Aram, and blessed him. [10] And God said to him, "Your name is Jacob; your name shall not be called Jacob anymore, but Israel shall be your name." So He called his name Israel. [11] Also God said to him: "I am God Almighty. Be fruitful and multiply; a nation and a company of nations shall proceed from you, and kings shall come from your body. [12] The land which I gave Abraham and Isaac I give to you; and to your descendants after you I give this land." [13] Then God went up from him in the place where He talked with him.

46:1-4

¹ So Israel took his journey with all that he had, and came to Beersheba, and offered sacrifices to the God of his father Isaac. ² Then God spoke to Israel in the visions of the night, and said, "Jacob, Jacob!"
And he said, "Here I am."
³ So He said, "I am God, the God of your father; do not fear to go down to Egypt, for I will make of you a great nation there. ⁴ I will go down with you to Egypt, and I will also surely bring you up again;

48:3-4

³ Then Jacob said to Joseph: "God Almighty appeared to me at Luz in the land of Canaan and blessed me, ⁴ and said to me, 'Behold, I will make you fruitful and multiply you, and I will make of you a multitude of people, and give this land to your descendants after you as an everlasting possession.'"

After Abraham died, one can see that the writer who continued writing the book, rarely mentions God and always says more or less the same thing, for example:

28:13-14

¹³ ... the land on which you lie I will give to you and your descendants. ¹⁴ Also your descendants shall be as the dust of the earth; you shall spread abroad to the west and the east, to the north and the south; and in you and in your seed all the families of the earth shall be blessed.

One could say that the great feat achieved in Genesis is that the writer, or writers, managed to create a great god! And they did so simply through endless repetition of the promise, by that unknown mysterious god, who promises once and again to a family emigrating from Aram to Canaan that he is a great god and will deliver unto Abraham and his descendants the land of Canaan forever. This formula repeats itself in Genesis and in the following books always in the same general form:

"I *am* the Lord God of Abraham your father and the God of Isaac; Your descendants shall be as the dust of the earth; you shall spread abroad to the west and the east. Then He said to him, "I *am* the Lord, who brought you out of Ur of the Chaldeans, to give you this land to inherit it. Look now toward heaven, and count the stars if you are able to number them." And He said to him, "So shall your descendants be."

We will keep following this formula, which will change slightly in subsequent books of the Torah. If we track this formula from the very beginning, we might notice that we still haven't received any logical explanation for it, which might make it sound a bit like brain washing.

So to summarize Genesis, I would just like to point out that even before the Bible humans believed in all kinds of gods, and this continues to this day. It seems it is a basic need of the human soul, to believe in something greater before which man can lay bare the yearnings of his heart, his ambitions,desires, and his wants, directly, without an intermediate. Each such god was adapted for a man's situation, his mental abilities or education. And this is the place to note that there are thousands of faiths and religions in the world, even more than there are languages, and obviously each person, without exception, is one hundred per cent certain that his faith and religion are the true and righteous way. Even those who read these pages will keep thinking, as in the past, that their faith and way is the right one, and all the rest are mere pagan beliefs and superstition. The greatest paradox in the world is that they're all right. From these we must exclude atheism, which is a movement that denies the existence of any god. This movement developed in the nineteenth century with the advancement of science and technology, and it seems it will continue gaining momentum until all pagan religions and faiths disappear from the face of the earth. But I want to reassure anyone who is apprehensive of that prospect that this could take a thousand years. But still, there are those who do not want such a movement to keep growing, so they got organized, each in their own way, to fight against it. A key method in the war on progress is weakening the general education system and putting emphasis on religious studies. Another method is increasing anti-Semitism in order to bring together the believers in their common hatred of the so-called true culprits. Incidentally, this method has been working for generations, and has been used as a successful distraction tactic for many harsh laws. Hatred among different ethnic groups can also be used as such a distraction technique.

I would like to immortalize here a friend, Alex, who experienced a very interesting anti-Semitic incident. It happened in one of the labor camps in the plains of Siberia. They were a group of eight prisoners who chopped down wood in the heart of the forest, under the supervision of a fellow prisoner, Vasili, who was a particularly violent type. The whole group was afraid of him because they could never predict his moods. The other prisoners were all peasants whose complete ignorance was the only thing they had in common.

As the only Jew in the group, Alex kept his faith secret and tried not to attract attention or get involved in anything. Alex was sure no one in the group knew he was Jewish. During one of their breaks everyone sat together under one of the trees. Vasili was the only one to tell various stories of his past in different work camps where he was prisoner. But for some reason Alex interrupted with a related comment and Vasili's anger was immediately ignited:

"Shut up! You disgusting Jew-face, I don't want to hear a word from you!".

Vanya, Vasili's good friend, who to the best of his knowledge had never met such a creature before, turned to Vasili and asked:

- "Vasili, are you sure that's a Jew?"
- "What, can you not see it on his face?"
- "But his face looks just like a human's!"

Exodus

1:21

[21] And so it was, because the midwives feared God, that He provided households for them.

I see this as one of the most important verses in the Torah (Pentateuch), maybe even the most important one! In the Torah, God, in all his glory, engages in building, which is why it must be the most important commandment in Judaism because it is the only one for which God sets a personal example

2:10

[10] And the child grew, and she brought him to Pharaoh's daughter, and he became her son. So she called his name Moses, saying, "Because I drew him out of the water." (Indeed, the Hebrew name sounds like the Hebrew for draw out.)

Pharaoh's daughter, it seems, knew Hebrew and for some reason preferred to name the child in Hebrew despite her father's hatred for and hostility towards the Jewish people. He hated the Jewish people with such vehemence that it could only be compared to Hitler; a hate that made Hitler assemble the best engineers and German minds in order to build special cities, and within them arrays of special ovens all in order to exterminate and burn the whole Jewish people. Hitler, who needed a system of trains in order to move his armies and their supplies across conquered Europe, preferred to collect and transport Jews from all the conquered countries to these slaughter cities to suffocate them in gas chambers.

3:6-8

⁶ "I am the God of your father—the God of Abraham, the God of Isaac, and the God of Jacob." And Moses hid his face, for he was afraid to look upon God.

⁷ And the Lord said: "I have surely seen the oppression of My people who are in Egypt, and have heard their cry because of their taskmasters, for I know their sorrows. ⁸ So I have come down to deliver them out of the hand of the Egyptians, and to bring them up from that land to a good and large land, to a land flowing with milk and honey, to the place of the Canaanites and the Hittites and the Amorites and the Perizzites and the Hivites and the Jebusites.

Six nations are listed here, who were all part of God's creation and lived in a good a large land with flowing milk and honey. Why would God want to squeeze a seventh people into such a small land when the whole of Planet Earth was at his disposal? Why would God want to annihilate all the peoples who lived in Canaan?

3:11-12

¹¹ But Moses said to God, "Who am I that I should go to Pharaoh, and that I should bring the children of Israel out of Egypt?"
¹² So He said, "I will certainly be with you. And this shall be a sign to you that I have sent you: When you have brought the people out of Egypt, you shall serve God on this mountain."

In no interpretation of the Bible have I found the meaning of this verse "you shall serve God on this mountain". How, what kind of service, why and for what? Also I see no connection, explanation or sign in this response.

3:15-22

[15] Moreover God said to Moses, "Thus you shall say to the children of Israel: 'The Lord God of your fathers, the God of Abraham, the God of Isaac, and the God of Jacob, has sent me to you. This is My name forever, and this is My memorial to all generations.' [16] Go and gather the elders of Israel together, and say to them, 'The Lord God of your fathers, the God of Abraham, of Isaac, and of Jacob, appeared to me, saying, "I have surely visited you and seen what is done to you in Egypt;[17] and I have said I will bring you up out of the affliction of Egypt to the land of the Canaanites and the Hittites and the Amorites and the Perizzites and the Hivites and the Jebusites, to a land flowing with milk and honey."' [18] Then they will heed your voice; and you shall come, you and the elders of Israel, to the king of Egypt; and you shall say to him, 'The Lord God of the Hebrews has met with us; and now, please, let us go three days' journey into the wilderness, that we may sacrifice to the Lord our God.' [19] But I am sure that the king of Egypt will not let you go, no, not even by a mighty hand. [20] So I will stretch out My hand and strike Egypt with all My wonders which I will do in its midst; and after that he will let you go. [21] And I will give this people favor in the sight of the Egyptians; and it shall be, when you go, that you shall not go empty-handed. [22] But every woman shall ask of her neighbor, namely, of her who dwells near her house, articles of silver, articles of gold, and clothing; and you shall put them on your sons and on your daughters. So you shall plunder the Egyptians."

Let's not forget that the Israelites who lived in Egypt at the time were all slaves. Could it be that the Egyptians who employed Hebrew slaves in their homes were so stupid, that they would lend clothes, silver and gold to their slaves? Or is this a continued attempt by the author to brainwash the reader, considering similar words that appear again in 11:2 and 12:31?

I must again point out that sacrifices at the altar are an ancient pagan custom which was common in all religions. This custom was created in order to please the gods, but mostly to provide free food for the priests and their families.

4:1-9

[1] Then Moses answered and said, "But suppose they will not believe me or listen to my voice; suppose they say, 'The Lord has not appeared to you.'"

[2] So the Lord said to him, "What is that in your hand?"

He said, "A rod."

[3] And He said, "Cast it on the ground." So he cast it on the ground, and it became a serpent; and Moses fled from it. [4] Then the Lord said to Moses, "Reach out your hand and take it by the tail" (and he reached out his hand and caught it, and it became a rod in his hand), [5] "that they may believe that the Lord God of their fathers, the God of Abraham, the God of Isaac, and the God of Jacob, has appeared to you."

[6] Furthermore the Lord said to him, "Now put your hand in your bosom." And he put his hand in his bosom, and when he took it out, behold, his hand was leprous, like snow. [7] And He said, "Put your hand in your bosom again." So he put his hand in his bosom again, and drew it out of his bosom, and behold, it was restored like his other flesh. [8] "Then it will be, if they do not believe you, nor heed the message of the first sign, that they may believe the message of the latter sign. [9] And it shall be, if they do not believe even these two signs, or listen to your voice, that you shall take water from the river and pour it on the dry land. The water which you take from the river will become blood on the dry land."

Again we witness sorcery, which God presumably teaches Moses. Considering all the Israelites of his time, who were slaves in the fullest sense of the word and labored and sweated every day of their lives, with no education, Moses was completely different! He grew up with the royal family. In those days Egypt was amoung the strongest and most developed nations in the world, even in their knowledge (see the pyramids). And Moses, who grew up among royalty, naturally received the best education that could be had at the time. He also learned all the tricks of the magicians of Egypt, and it seems he was an excellent student because he performed tricks that even the magicians of Egypt couldn't outdo.

4:10-17

[10] Then Moses said to the Lord, "O my Lord, I am not eloquent, neither before nor since You have spoken to Your servant; but I am slow of speech and slow of tongue."
[11] So the Lord said to him, "Who has made man's mouth? Or who makes the mute, the deaf, the seeing, or the blind? Have not I, the Lord? [12] Now therefore, go, and I will be with your mouth and teach you what you shall say."
[13] But he said, "O my Lord, please send by the hand of whomever else You may send."
[14] So the anger of the Lord was kindled against Moses, and He said: "Is not Aaron the Levite your brother? I know that he can speak well. And look, he is also coming out to meet you. When he sees you, he will be glad in his heart. [15] Now you shall speak to him and put the words in his mouth. And I will be with your mouth and with his mouth, and I will teach you what you shall do. [16] So he shall be your spokesman to the people. And he himself shall be as a mouth for you, and you shall be to him as God.[17] And you shall take this rod in your hand, with which you shall do the signs."

God, who could easily resolve Moses' stutter, chooses to complicate things and makes stuttering Moses explain God's will to his brother Aaron who will then pass his words along to the people. God reminds Moses not to forget the rod when he goes to see Pharaoh, the rod without which the tricks of sorcery cannot be performed.

4:21

[21] And the LORD said to Moses, "When you go back to Egypt, see that you do all those wonders before Pharaoh which

I have put in your hand. But I will harden his heart, so that he will not let the people go.

God reminds Moses again of the sorcery that he supposedly taught him. I cannot understand why God wanted to harden Pharaoh's heart; so that he wouldn't let the people go immediately? If he had the power to harden his heart, why not soften it instead of delaying the liberation of the people from their hard labor? This makes one think again that this is a children's story.

4:24

²⁴ And it came to pass on the way, at the encampment, that the LORD met him and sought to kill him.

This verse completely contradicts all that happened between God and Moses. Contradicts all the promises and covenants that God made Moses since they first met.

4:27-31

²⁷ And the LORD said to Aaron, "Go into the wilderness to meet Moses." So he went and met him on the mountain of God, and kissed him. ²⁸ So Moses told Aaron all the words of the LORD who had sent him, and all the signs which He had commanded him. ²⁹ Then Moses and Aaron went and gathered together all the elders of the children of Israel. ³⁰ And Aaron spoke all the words which the LORD had spoken to Moses. Then he did the signs in the sight of the people. ³¹ So the people believed; and when they heard that the LORD had visited the children of Israel and that He had looked on their affliction, then they bowed their heads and worshipped.

Moses teaches Aaron all of his magic tricks and together they practice sorcery in front of elders of Israel, before they go to Pharaoh. And indeed they managed to convince their elders that God is on their side.

5:1-14

¹ Afterward Moses and Aaron went in and told Pharaoh, "Thus says the LORD God of Israel: 'Let My people go, that they may hold a feast to Me in the wilderness.'"

² And Pharaoh said, "Who is the LORD, that I should obey His voice to let Israel go? I do not know the LORD, nor will I let Israel go."

³ So they said, "The God of the Hebrews has met with us. Please, let us go three days' journey into the desert and sacrifice to the LORD our God, lest He fall upon us with pestilence or with the sword."

⁴ Then the king of Egypt said to them, "Moses and Aaron, why do you take the people from their work? Get back to your labor." ⁵ And Pharaoh said, "Look, the people of the land are many now, and you make them rest from their labor!"

⁶ So the same day Pharaoh commanded the taskmasters of the people and their officers, saying, ⁷ "You shall no longer give the people straw to make bricks as before. Let them go and gather straw for themselves. ⁸ And you shall lay on them the quota of bricks which they made before. You shall not reduce it. For they are idle; therefore they cry out, saying, 'Let us go and sacrifice to our God.' ⁹ Let more work be laid on the men, that they may labor in it, and let them not regard false words."

¹⁰ And the taskmasters of the people and their officers went out and spoke to the people, saying, "Thus says Pharaoh: 'I will not give you straw. ¹¹ Go, get yourselves straw where you can find it; yet none of your work will be reduced.'" ¹² So the people were scattered abroad throughout all the land of Egypt to gather stubble instead of straw. ¹³ And the taskmasters forced them to hurry, saying, "Fulfill your work, your daily quota, as when there was straw." ¹⁴ Also the officers of the children of Israel, whom Pharaoh's taskmasters had set over them, were beaten and were asked, "Why have you not fulfilled your task in making bricks both yesterday and today, as before?"

5:22-23

²² So Moses returned to the LORD and said, "Lord, why have You brought trouble on this people? Why is it You have sent me? ²³ For since I came to Pharaoh to speak in Your name, he has done evil to this people; neither have You delivered Your people at all."

6:7-8

⁷ "I will take you as My people, and I will be your God. Then you shall know that I am the LORD your God who brings you out from under the burdens of the Egyptians. ⁸ And I will bring you into the land which I swore to give to Abraham, Isaac, and Jacob; and I will give it to you as a heritage: I am the LORD."

6:12

¹² And Moses spoke before the LORD, saying, "The children of Israel have not heeded me. How then shall Pharaoh heed me, for I am of uncircumcised lips?"

6:28-30

²⁸ And it came to pass, on the day the LORD spoke to Moses in the land of Egypt, ²⁹ that the LORD spoke to Moses, saying, "I am the LORD. Speak to Pharaoh king of Egypt all that I say to you."
³⁰ But Moses said before the LORD, "Behold, I am of uncircumcised lips, and how shall Pharaoh heed me?"

7:1-5

¹ So the LORD said to Moses: "See, I have made you as God to Pharaoh, and Aaron your brother shall be your prophet. ² You shall speak all that I command you. And Aaron your

brother shall tell Pharaoh to send the children of Israel out of his land. ³ And I will harden Pharaoh's heart, and multiply My signs and My wonders in the land of Egypt. ⁴ But Pharaoh will not heed you, so that I may lay My hand on Egypt and bring My armies and My people, the children of Israel, out of the land of Egypt by great judgments. ⁵ And the Egyptians shall know that I am the LORD, when I stretch out My hand on Egypt and bring out the children of Israel from among them."

Up until now in order for Moses to see God, he had to wait until God appeared before him, but a major change took place and all this has changed. It seems God has chambers, and whenever Moses needs God he simply walks into his chambers and lays out his claims. Another change is that God appoint the slaves who are about to be set free, as his army.

7:8-13

⁸ Then the LORD spoke to Moses and Aaron, saying, ⁹ "When Pharaoh speaks to you, saying, 'Show a miracle for yourselves,' then you shall say to Aaron, 'Take your rod and cast it before Pharaoh, and let it become a serpent.'" ¹⁰ So Moses and Aaron went in to Pharaoh, and they did so, just as the LORD commanded. And Aaron cast down his rod before Pharaoh and before his servants, and it became a serpent.
¹¹ But Pharaoh also called the wise men and the sorcerers; so the magicians of Egypt, they also did in like manner with their enchantments. ¹² For every man threw down his rod, and they became serpents. But Aaron's rod swallowed up their rods. ¹³ And Pharaoh's heart grew hard, and he did not heed them, as the LORD had said.

God tells Moses and Aaron that if Pharaoh asks for proof that their god exists, Aaron should throw his rod down at Pharaoh's feet and the rod will turn into a serpent.

7:14-16

[14] So the LORD said to Moses: "Pharaoh's heart is hard; he refuses to let the people go. [15] Go to Pharaoh in the morning, when he goes out to the water, and you shall stand by the river's bank to meet him; and the rod which was turned to a serpent you shall take in your hand. [16] And you shall say to him, 'The LORD God of the Hebrews has sent me to you, saying, "Let My people go, that they may serve Me in the wilderness"; but indeed, until now you would not hear!'"

7:17-24

[17] Thus says the LORD: "By this you shall know that I am the LORD. Behold, I will strike the waters which are in the river with the rod that is in my hand, and they shall be turned to blood. [18] And the fish that are in the river shall die, the river shall stink, and the Egyptians will loathe to drink the water of the river."'
[19] Then the LORD spoke to Moses, "Say to Aaron, 'Take your rod and stretch out your hand over the waters of Egypt, over their streams, over their rivers, over their ponds, and over all their pools of water, that they may become blood.' And there shall be blood throughout all the land of Egypt, both in buckets of wood and pitchers of stone." [20] And Moses and Aaron did so, just as the LORD commanded. So he lifted up the rod and struck the waters that were in the river, in the sight of Pharaoh and in the sight of his servants. And all the waters that were in the river were turned to blood. [21] The fish that were in the river died, the river stank, and the Egyptians could not drink the water of the river. So there was blood throughout all the land of Egypt.
[22] Then the magicians of Egypt did so with their enchantments; and Pharaoh's heart grew hard, and he did not heed them, as the LORD had said. [23] And Pharaoh turned and went into his house. Neither was his heart moved by this. [24] So all the Egyptians dug all around the river for water to drink, because they could not drink the water of the river.

This last task was indeed very difficult on Moses and Aaron. Anyone who is familiar with the geography of Egypt knows that it is a large country, so in order to reach all the streams and rivers, lakes and water sources and hit each and every one with the magic rod, would indeed be a difficult and amazing task, if not entirely impossible, especially considering their age.

[7] And Moses was eighty years old and Aaron eighty-three years old when they spoke to Pharaoh.

And to this we can add their next assignment:

7:25-8:4

[25] And seven days passed after the LORD had struck the river.
[1] And the LORD spoke to Moses, "Go to Pharaoh and say to him, 'Thus says the LORD: "Let My people go, that they may serve Me. [2] But if you refuse to let them go, behold, I will smite all your territory with frogs. [3] So the river shall bring forth frogs abundantly, which shall go up and come into your house, into your bedroom, on your bed, into the houses of your servants, on your people, into your ovens, and into your kneading bowls. [4] And the frogs shall come up on you, on your people, and on all your servants."'"

8:5-15

[5] Then the LORD spoke to Moses, "Say to Aaron, 'Stretch out your hand with your rod over the streams, over the rivers, and over the ponds, and cause frogs to come up on the land of Egypt.'" [6] So Aaron stretched out his hand over the waters of Egypt, and the frogs came up and covered the land of Egypt. [7] And the magicians did so with their enchantments, and brought up frogs on the land of Egypt.
[8] Then Pharaoh called for Moses and Aaron, and said, "Entreat the LORD that He may take away the frogs from me

and from my people; and I will let the people go, that they may sacrifice to the LORD."

⁹ And Moses said to Pharaoh, "Accept the honor of saying when I shall intercede for you, for your servants, and for your people, to destroy the frogs from you and your houses, that they may remain in the river only."

¹⁰ So he said, "Tomorrow." And he said, "Let it be according to your word, that you may know that there is no one like the LORD our God. ¹¹ And the frogs shall depart from you, from your houses, from your servants, and from your people. They shall remain in the river only."

¹² Then Moses and Aaron went out from Pharaoh. And Moses cried out to the LORD concerning the frogs which He had brought against Pharaoh. ¹³ So the LORD did according to the word of Moses. And the frogs died out of the houses, out of the courtyards, and out of the fields. ¹⁴ They gathered them together in heaps, and the land stank. ¹⁵ But when Pharaoh saw that there was relief, he hardened his heart and did not heed them, as the LORD had said.

8:16-19

¹⁶ So the LORD said to Moses, "Say to Aaron, 'Stretch out your rod, and strike the dust of the land, so that it may become lice throughout all the land of Egypt.'" ¹⁷ And they did so. For Aaron stretched out his hand with his rod and struck the dust of the earth, and it became lice on man and beast. All the dust of the land became lice throughout all the land of Egypt.

¹⁸ Now the magicians so worked with their enchantments to bring forth lice, but they could not. So there were lice on man and beast. ¹⁹ Then the magicians said to Pharaoh, "This is the finger of God." But Pharaoh's heart grew hard, and he did not heed them, just as the LORD had said.

8:20-32

²⁰ And the LORD said to Moses, "Rise early in the morning and stand before Pharaoh as he comes out to the water. Then

say to him, 'Thus says the LORD: "Let My people go, that they may serve Me. ²¹ Or else, if you will not let My people go, behold, I will send swarms of flies on you and your servants, on your people and into your houses. The houses of the Egyptians shall be full of swarms of flies, and also the ground on which they stand. ²² And in that day I will set apart the land of Goshen, in which My people dwell, that no swarms of flies shall be there, in order that you may know that I am the LORD in the midst of the land. ²³ I will make a difference[a] between My people and your people. Tomorrow this sign shall be." '" ²⁴ And the LORD did so. Thick swarms of flies came into the house of Pharaoh, into his servants' houses, and into all the land of Egypt. The land was corrupted because of the swarms of flies.

²⁵ Then Pharaoh called for Moses and Aaron, and said, "Go, sacrifice to your God in the land."

²⁶ And Moses said, "It is not right to do so, for we would be sacrificing the abomination of the Egyptians to the LORD our God. If we sacrifice the abomination of the Egyptians before their eyes, then will they not stone us? ²⁷ We will go three days' journey into the wilderness and sacrifice to the LORD our God as He will command us."

²⁸ So Pharaoh said, "I will let you go, that you may sacrifice to the LORD your God in the wilderness; only you shall not go very far away. Intercede for me."

²⁹ Then Moses said, "Indeed I am going out from you, and I will entreat the LORD, that the swarms of flies may depart tomorrow from Pharaoh, from his servants, and from his people. But let Pharaoh not deal deceitfully anymore in not letting the people go to sacrifice to the LORD."

³⁰ So Moses went out from Pharaoh and entreated the LORD. ³¹ And the LORD did according to the word of Moses; He removed the swarms of flies from Pharaoh, from his servants, and from his people. Not one remained. ³² But Pharaoh hardened his heart at this time also; neither would he let the people go.

9:1-7

Then the LORD said to Moses, "Go in to Pharaoh and tell him, 'Thus says the LORD God of the Hebrews: "Let My people go, that they may serve Me. ² For if you refuse to let them go, and still hold them, ³ behold, the hand of the LORD will be on your cattle in the field, on the horses, on the donkeys, on the camels, on the oxen, and on the sheep—a very severe pestilence. ⁴ And the LORD will make a difference between the livestock of Israel and the livestock of Egypt. So nothing shall die of all that belongs to the children of Israel."'" ⁵ Then the LORD appointed a set time, saying, "Tomorrow the LORD will do this thing in the land."
⁶ So the LORD did this thing on the next day, and all the livestock of Egypt died; but of the livestock of the children of Israel, not one died. ⁷ Then Pharaoh sent, and indeed, not even one of the livestock of the Israelites was dead. But the heart of Pharaoh became hard, and he did not let the people go.

9:1

¹ Then the LORD said to Moses, "Go in to Pharaoh and tell him, 'Thus says the LORD God of the Hebrews ... '"

This verse states that the Lord (Jehovah) is actually the god of only a particular group – meaning a pagan god! The god of a large group of slaves that lived under the oppression of the Egyptians.

9:8-12

⁸ So the LORD said to Moses and Aaron, "Take for yourselves handfuls of ashes from a furnace, and let Moses scatter it toward the heavens in the sight of Pharaoh. ⁹ And it will become fine dust in all the land of Egypt, and it will cause boils that break out in sores on man and beast throughout all the land of Egypt." ¹⁰ Then they took ashes from the furnace and stood before Pharaoh, and Moses scattered them toward

heaven. And they caused boils that break out in sores on man and beast. [11] And the magicians could not stand before Moses because of the boils, for the boils were on the magicians and on all the Egyptians. [12] But the LORD hardened the heart of Pharaoh; and he did not heed them, just as the LORD had spoken to Moses.

When reading the chapters about the contest between the Egyptian magicians and Moses and Aaron who were guided by God, one at first gets the false impression that it is merely a children's story. But on further examination one notices that it's a story of a collision between two forces: the force of God defeats the powers of Pharaoh and his magicians in order to prove that the Lord is the supreme God, and later that he is also the only god. And history has shown that this has happened. The belief in the Lord stuck in the minds of the people whom Moses led through the desert. Not for nothing did Moses choose Egypt as a suitable adversary for God. Egypt, which was the closest, strongest and best-known super-power in the region, indeed seems to Moses to be a proper match for God.

10:2

[2] And that you may tell in the hearing of your son and your son's son the mighty things I have done in Egypt ...

Again we witness a pagan god created by man with the characteristics of man. The only animal on the planet that enjoys abusing its own is man, though for some reason it is considered to be smarter

10:21-26

[21] Then the LORD said to Moses, "Stretch out your hand toward heaven, that there may be darkness over the land of Egypt, darkness which may even be felt." [22] So Moses stretched out his hand toward heaven, and there was thick

darkness in all the land of Egypt three days. [23] They did not see one another; nor did anyone rise from his place for three days. But all the children of Israel had light in their dwellings.

[24] Then Pharaoh called to Moses and said, "Go, serve the LORD; only let your flocks and your herds be kept back. Let your little ones also go with you."

[25] But Moses said, "You must also give us sacrifices and burnt offerings, that we may sacrifice to the LORD our God. [26] Our livestock also shall go with us; not a hoof shall be left behind. For we must take some of them to serve the LORD our God, and even we do not know with what we must serve the LORD until we arrive there."

In all my life, to this day, I could never understand what 'serving god' means. But today, after reading that even Moses, who reinvented God, did not know how to serve him, I feel at at ease.

11:1-3

[1] And the LORD said to Moses, "I will bring one more plague on Pharaoh and on Egypt. Afterward he will let you go from here. When he lets you go, he will surely drive you out of here altogether. [2] Speak now in the hearing of the people, and let every man ask from his neighbor and every woman from her neighbor, articles of silver and articles of gold." [3] And the LORD gave the people favor in the sight of the Egyptians.

12:14-15

[14] 'So this day shall be to you a memorial; and you shall keep it as a feast to the LORD throughout your generations. You shall keep it as a feast by an everlasting ordinance. [15] Seven days you shall eat unleavened bread. On the first day you shall remove leaven from your houses. For whoever eats leavened bread from the first day until the seventh day, that person shall be cut off from Israel.

12:35-37

35 Now the children of Israel had done according to the word of Moses, and they had asked from the Egyptians articles of silver, articles of gold, and clothing. **36** And the LORD had given the people favor in the sight of the Egyptians, so that they granted them what they requested. Thus they plundered the Egyptians.

37 Then the children of Israel journeyed from Rameses to Succoth, about six hundred thousand men on foot, besides children.

13:18

18 So God led the people around by way of the wilderness of the Red Sea. And the children of Israel went up in orderly ranks out of the land of Egypt.

It would seem that the rich Egyptians, who owned silver and gold items, were rather neighborly with their beleaguered slaves. However, I don't understand why God would want the slaves leaving Egypt to rob their Egyptian neighbors. And since this phrase appears in Exodus alone more times than 'you shall not steal' appears in the entire Bible, I get the impression that this great robbery of Egyptian valuables was carefully planned by Moses so *he* could take all the gold when the time came. In order to arm six hundred thousand infantry today with such weapons as bows and arrows, swords and shields, one would need several arms factories, working non-stop for months. Here no doubt the writer let his imagination run wild. To say nothing of the Egyptians who took no notice of this great effort: the manufacturing of arms and the arming of the Hebrew slaves (who didn't know how to use these weapons).

17:8-14

⁸ Now Amalek came and fought with Israel in Rephidim. ⁹ And Moses said to Joshua, "Choose us some men and go out, fight with Amalek. Tomorrow I will stand on the top of the hill with the rod of God in my hand." ¹⁰ So Joshua did as Moses said to him, and fought with Amalek. And Moses, Aaron, and Hur went up to the top of the hill. ¹¹ And so it was, when Moses held up his hand, that Israel prevailed; and when he let down his hand, Amalek prevailed. ¹² But Moses's hands became heavy; so they took a stone and put it under him, and he sat on it. And Aaron and Hur supported his hands, one on one side, and the other on the other side; and his hands were steady until the going down of the sun. ¹³ So Joshua defeated Amalek and his people with the edge of the sword.
¹⁴ Then the LORD said to Moses, "Write this for a memorial in the book and recount it in the hearing of Joshua, that I will utterly blot out the remembrance of Amalek from under heaven."

This was the Israelites' first encounter with an attacking army. God asks Moses to chronicle the outcome of this battle.

19:1-9

¹ In the third month after the children of Israel had gone out of the land of Egypt, on the same day, they came to the Wilderness of Sinai. ² For they had departed from Rephidim, had come to the Wilderness of Sinai, and camped in the wilderness. So Israel camped there before the mountain.
³ And Moses went up to God, and the LORD called to him from the mountain, saying, "Thus you shall say to the house of Jacob, and tell the children of Israel: ⁴ 'You have seen what I did to the Egyptians, and how I bore you on eagles' wings and brought you to Myself. ⁵ Now therefore, if you will indeed obey My voice and keep My covenant, then you shall be a special treasure to Me above all people; for all the earth is Mine. ⁶ And you shall be to Me a kingdom of priests and a

holy nation.' These are the words which you shall speak to the children of Israel."

⁷ So Moses came and called for the elders of the people, and laid before them all these words which the LORD commanded him. ⁸ Then all the people answered together and said, "All that the LORD has spoken we will do." So Moses brought back the words of the people to the LORD. ⁹ And the LORD said to Moses, "Behold, I come to you in the thick cloud, that the people may hear when I speak with you, and believe you forever."

So Moses told the words of the people to the LORD.

19:10-25

¹⁰ Then the LORD said to Moses, "Go to the people and consecrate them today and tomorrow, and let them wash their clothes. ¹¹ And let them be ready for the third day. For on the third day the LORD will come down upon Mount Sinai in the sight of all the people. ¹² You shall set bounds for the people all around, saying, 'Take heed to yourselves that you do not go up to the mountain or touch its base. Whoever touches the mountain shall surely be put to death. ¹³ Not a hand shall touch him, but he shall surely be stoned or shot with an arrow; whether man or beast, he shall not live.' When the trumpet sounds long, they shall come near the mountain."

¹⁴ So Moses went down from the mountain to the people and sanctified the people, and they washed their clothes. ¹⁵ And he said to the people, "Be ready for the third day; do not come near your wives."

¹⁶ Then it came to pass on the third day, in the morning, that there were thunderings and lightnings, and a thick cloud on the mountain; and the sound of the trumpet was very loud, so that all the people who were in the camp trembled. ¹⁷ And Moses brought the people out of the camp to meet with God, and they stood at the foot of the mountain. ¹⁸ Now Mount Sinai was completely in smoke, because the LORD descended upon it in fire. Its smoke ascended like the smoke of a furnace, and the whole mountain quaked greatly. ¹⁹ And when the blast of the

trumpet sounded long and became louder and louder, Moses spoke, and God answered him by voice. [20] Then the LORD came down upon Mount Sinai, on the top of the mountain. And the LORD called Moses to the top of the mountain, and Moses went up.

[21] And the LORD said to Moses, "Go down and warn the people, lest they break through to gaze at the LORD, and many of them perish. [22] Also let the priests who come near the LORD consecrate themselves, lest the LORD break out against them."

[23] But Moses said to the LORD, "The people cannot come up to Mount Sinai; for You warned us, saying, 'Set bounds around the mountain and consecrate it.'"

[24] Then the LORD said to him, "Away! Get down and then come up, you and Aaron with you. But do not let the priests and the people break through to come up to the LORD, lest He break out against them." [25] So Moses went down to the people and spoke to them.

A trend clearly develops, where Moses continually changes the form of God – the same god who created man in his image. After all, anyone can show up and say "I am the Lord God", and people would be hard pressed to accept it. But humbly saying "I am God's messenger" is easier to accept. True, Abraham created God in his hallucinations, but Moses, an erudite person, far more educated than most, decided to recreate God. First he purportedly sees him as a burning bush in the desert, but this wouldn't impress the rabble trekking through the desert; God needs to be sublime. So Moses turns to the elders who can be easily convinced (as has been shown time and again to this day). He arranges for God to appear in a cloud, and tells the people that in three days' time God will appear before them, but they must first wash their clothes and cannot go near their wives during those three days. It seems women are still held accountable for that serpent and tree of knowledge business, when woman was responsible for man's opening his eyes and facing reality.

Early in the morning of the third day, the people wake up, startled by thunder and lightning and the loud sound of a ram's horn, possibly several ram horns. Heavy smoke covers the mountain. And out of the smoke God calls to Moses to climb the mountain. Like every dictator, Moses too has a private army of no mean proportions, that is at his beck and call. Without his army Moses could not have survived. Moses placed his men – all covered in smoke from an earlier fire of non-dry bushes – just a short way up from the foot of the mountain. Already during the night, along with his other preparations, Moses took care of engulfing the mountain in smoke emanating from burning bushes. Moses instructed his men to stone or shoot arrows at any curious person trying to scale the mountain, after having warned the people not to even think of it. Moses has now turned the Lord into a god that no one can see, and anyone who does catch a glimpse of him is sure to die instantly – and who would want to die?

Despite Moses's extensive mastery of illusions and sleight of hand, he could not keep his promise that all the people would be able to see God. He therefore changes tack, claiming that God would not allow anyone to climb the mountain because it is a holy place, and that whoever sees the Lord will die – a new threat. Turns out that the people did not take Moses's word for it that the Lord God even existed. In those days anyone could buy as many gods as they wanted in the local household goods-and-gods shop. Every home had gods of various shapes and forms, and if you didn't want to buy a god, you could make one yourself out of clay, gold, or even mud. So it was very difficult to convince the people that only one god existed and that he alone is the one true God. To this day these persuasion efforts continue all over the world, and yet there are still thousands of religions and faiths!

Next, Moses comes down from the mountain to face his people, with the codex that was ostensibly given to him by God, but which Moses had prepared in advance. This codex is a collection of basic laws, some of which were common among many tribes and people that lived in the region, and some were humane laws devised by Moses, through which he hoped to rule the people. In my opinion, Moses's real wish was to become a god himself, but for reasons mentioned earlier in this chapter he compromised and remained the messenger of God, which is no easy task in and of itself. Moses therefore invests huge efforts in aggrandizing his god, Jehovah, so that he himself is not perceived as merely a minor messenger, but a messenger of a supreme god! Indeed, he was successful. Even today, thousands of years after the events recounted in the Torah, Moses is considered the most important messenger ever sent by the supreme god Jehovah to liberate the Israelites from slavery – with God's help, of course.

Humbly, I have added a few very important commandments, to update the codex for the twenty-first century.

The Ten Commandments

Exodus 20:3-17

³ "You shall have no other gods before Me.

⁴ You shall not make for yourself a carved image—any likeness of anything that is in heaven above, or that is in the earth beneath, or that is in the water under the earth; ⁵ you shall not bow down to them nor serve them. For I, the LORD your God, am a jealous God, visiting the iniquity of the fathers upon the children to the third and fourth generations of those who hate Me, ⁶ but showing mercy to thousands, to those who love Me and keep My commandments.

⁷ You shall not take the name of the LORD your God in vain, for the LORD will not hold him guiltless who takes His name in vain.

⁸ Remember the Sabbath day, to keep it holy. ⁹ Six days you shall labor and do all your work, ¹⁰ but the seventh day is the Sabbath of the LORD your God. In it you shall do no work: you, nor your son, nor your daughter, nor your male servant, nor your female servant, nor your cattle, nor your stranger who is within your gates. ¹¹ For in six days the LORD made the heavens and the earth, the sea, and all that is in them, and rested the seventh day. Therefore the LORD blessed the Sabbath day and hallowed it.

¹² Honor your father and your mother, that your days may be long upon the land which the LORD your God is giving you.

¹³ You shall not murder.

¹⁴ You shall not commit adultery.

¹⁵ You shall not steal.

¹⁶ You shall not bear false witness against your neighbor.

¹⁷ You shall not covet your neighbor's house; you shall not covet your neighbor's wife, nor his male servant, nor his female servant, nor his ox, nor his donkey, nor anything that is your neighbor's."

You shall not hate your friend, neighbor, and fellow man because the color of his skin is lighter or darker than yours.

You shall not hate anyone just because he is poorer or richer, uglier or prettier, smarter or dumber than you.

For the Chosen (Jewish) People only:

You shall not hate Sephardic Jews, Ashkenazi Jews, Yemenites, Moroccans, Kurds, Romanians, Poles, Russians, Arabs, Orthodox Jews, Secular Jews, intellectuals and those who were born to be ignorant. Stop hating!!!

20:18-21

[18] Now all the people witnessed the thunderings, the lightning flashes, the sound of the trumpet, and the mountain smoking; and when the people saw it, they trembled and stood afar off. [19] Then they said to Moses, "You speak with us, and we will hear; but let not God speak with us, lest we die."

[20] And Moses said to the people, "Do not fear; for God has come to test you, and that His fear may be before you, so that you may not sin." [21] So the people stood afar off, but Moses drew near the thick darkness where God was.

Moses's success was far and beyond expectations, he accomplished his goal and hoped for social peace as he continued to lead the Israelites.

20:22-26

[22] Then the LORD said to Moses, "Thus you shall say to the children of Israel: 'You have seen that I have talked with you from heaven. [23] You shall not make anything to be with Me— gods of silver or gods of gold you shall not make for yourselves. [24] An altar of earth you shall make for Me, and you shall sacrifice on it your burnt offerings and your peace offerings, your sheep and your oxen. In every place where I record My name I will come to you, and I will bless you. [25] And if you make Me an altar of stone, you shall not build it of

hewn stone; for if you use your tool on it, you have profaned it. [26] Nor shall you go up by steps to My altar, that your nakedness may not be exposed on it.'

One gets the impression that God loved to eat huge quantities of meat – quantities that could have fed Moses' private army. If it weren't for the verse "Nor shall you go up by steps to My altar, that your nakedness may not be exposed on it" we might have taken the other verses more seriously.

21:1-6

[1]"Now these are the judgments which you shall set before them: [2] If you buy a Hebrew servant, he shall serve six years; and in the seventh he shall go out free and pay nothing. [3] If he comes in by himself, he shall go out by himself; if he comes in married, then his wife shall go out with him. [4] If his master has given him a wife, and she has borne him sons or daughters, the wife and her children shall be her master's, and he shall go out by himself. [5] But if the servant plainly says, 'I love my master, my wife, and my children; I will not go out free,' [6] then his master shall bring him to the judges. He shall also bring him to the door, or to the doorpost, and his master shall pierce his ear with an awl; and he shall serve him forever.

I cannot understand how the Lord, God of Abraham, God of Isaac, and God of Jacob who had brought us as slaves out of Egypt, with a strong hand and outstretched arm to live as a free people, now instructs Moses about how Hebrew slaves should be treated. Moreover, it was very important to Moses to set it down in writing, as though it's a continuation of the Ten Commandments. This makes it clear that even as the Israelites left Egypt their slavery continued, and continues to this day. So I must proclaim here and now:

The Lord God is not a slaver!!
Man, who was created in God's image, was born free!!!

Simply writing these rules immediately after the Ten Commandments is an insufferable insult and is disrespectful to God. Over the years, hundreds of thousands of books, and more, were written that try to explain God's words – all providing different opinions and explanations for words that never came from God. When reading the Ten Commandments you can clearly see that they were written in simple language (even in the original Hebrew), so there is no need to explain or interpret them. Anyone can follow them without any difficulty after acquiring the most basic Hebrew. Not only that, but one mustn't explain or interpret the words of God – never, no one – it is the worst kind of condescension and offense to God. The man who knows and follows all the commandments is a good person all around and of course a giant in the Torah!

24:1-2

¹Now He said to Moses, "Come up to the LORD, you and Aaron, Nadab and Abihu, and seventy of the elders of Israel, and worship from afar. ² And Moses alone shall come near the LORD, but they shall not come near; nor shall the people go up with him."

Moses respects Israel's elders; when he invites them to join a meeting with God he asks them to worship Him from afar while only he approaches on his own. This shows how Moses succeeds in creating and imposing class distinctions.

24:5-8

⁵ Then he sent young men of the children of Israel, who offered burnt offerings and sacrificed peace offerings of oxen to the LORD. ⁶ And Moses took half the blood and put it in basins, and half the blood he sprinkled on the altar. ⁷ Then he took the Book of the Covenant and read in the hearing of the people. And they said, "All that the LORD has said, we will do, and be obedient." ⁸ And Moses took the blood, sprinkled it on

the people, and said, "This is the blood of the covenant which the LORD has made with you according to all these words."

Moses wrote down all his thoughts and musings even when he was a student in Egypt. As an educated man he kept all these writings in a book, which later he was able to call the Book of the Covenant and from which he read the Ten Commandments for example, or other humane laws he learned or heard of that were common among other nations. After the recent events, it seems that the group of people Moses led through the desert had complete faith in him. And here Moses sees fit to perform a full-fledged pagan rite in order to impress the Israelites, who were a collection of primitive people.

24:9-11

[9] Then Moses went up, also Aaron, Nadab, and Abihu, and seventy of the elders of Israel, [10] and they saw the God of Israel. And there was under His feet as it were a paved work of sapphire stone, and it was like the very heavens in its clarity. [11] But on the nobles of the children of Israel He did not lay His hand. So they saw God, and they ate and drank.

This description explains verse 24:5 – why oxen were sacrificed to God. The event was a kind of conference of top officers which included a good meal, barbeque, and drinks; all while watching the vision of God appear with a pavement of sapphire stone under his feet as blue as the sky. This particular appearance of God is not explained anywhere.

24:17-18

[17] The sight of the glory of the LORD was like a consuming fire on the top of the mountain in the eyes of the children of Israel. [18] So Moses went into the midst of the cloud and went up into the mountain. And Moses was on the mountain forty days and forty nights.

Again Moses chooses to change the form of God, no more 'So God created man in His own image; in the image of God He created him; male and female He created them.' Now God is stronger and scarier, cloaked in fire and smoke, a God that not everyone would want or could see, because anyone who saw God would be killed. But if we look at 24:11 we will see that it says:

[11] But on the nobles of the children of Israel He did not lay *His hand*.

It seems Moses has a hard time letting go of old habits. After a lot of hard work, Moses decides to take a lengthy vacation, to sit in solitude and think of new ideas that were not yet in his book.

25:1-7

[1] Then the LORD spoke to Moses, saying: [2] "Speak to the children of Israel, that they bring Me an offering. From everyone who gives it willingly with his heart you shall take My offering. [3] And this is the offering which you shall take from them: gold, silver and bronze; [4] blue, purple and scarlet thread, fine linen, and goats' hair; [5] ram skins dyed red, badger skins and acacia wood; [6] oil for the light and spices for the anointing oil and for the sweet incense; [7] onyx stones and stones to be set in the ephod and in the breastplate.

25:8-22

[8] "And let them make Me a sanctuary, that I may dwell among them. [9] According to all that I show you, that is, the pattern of the tabernacle and the pattern of all its furnishings, just so you shall make it.
[10] "And they shall make an ark of acacia wood; two and a half cubits shall be its length, a cubit and a half its width, and a cubit and a half its height. [11] And you shall overlay it with pure gold, inside and out you shall overlay it, and shall make on it a

molding of gold all around. ¹² You shall cast four rings of gold for it, and put them in its four corners; two rings shall be on one side, and two rings on the other side. ¹³ And you shall make poles of acacia wood, and overlay them with gold. ¹⁴ You shall put the poles into the rings on the sides of the ark, that the ark may be carried by them. ¹⁵ The poles shall be in the rings of the ark; they shall not be taken from it. ¹⁶ And you shall put into the ark the Testimony which I will give you.

¹⁷ "You shall make a mercy seat of pure gold; two and a half cubits shall be its length and a cubit and a half its width. ¹⁸ And you shall make two cherubim of gold; of hammered work, you shall make them at the two ends of the mercy seat. ¹⁹ Make one cherub at one end, and the other cherub at the other end; you shall make the cherubim at the two ends of it of one piece with the mercy seat. ²⁰ And the cherubim shall stretch out their wings above, covering the mercy seat with their wings, and they shall face one another; the faces of the cherubim shall be toward the mercy seat. ²¹ You shall put the mercy seat on top of the ark, and in the ark you shall put the Testimony that I will give you. ²² And there I will meet with you, and I will speak with you from above the mercy seat, from between the two cherubim which are on the ark of the Testimony, about everything which I will give you in commandment to the children of Israel."

These are the instructions God gives to Moses for building a crate of these exact measurements, where God will reside when he appears in the temple. Based on these dimensions, which God himself ordered, it seems God was rather compact. I do not know why Moses chooses to build such a small crate for carrying God from place to place that would be connected by two gold rings on each side. God, who built the whole world in six days merely with his words, and who can move quickly between all the worlds in the universe, asks for a box suitable for a dwarf in which to rest and be transported from place to place while he visits the tabernacle. If this is not disrespectful to God and his followers then what is? However, this section seems to contain a logical argument for the non-existence of the Lord God altogether.

25:23-30

[23] "You shall also make a table of acacia wood; two cubits shall be its length, a cubit its width, and a cubit and a half its height. [24] And you shall overlay it with pure gold, and make a molding of gold all around. [25] You shall make for it a frame of a handbreadth all around, and you shall make a gold molding for the frame all around. [26] And you shall make for it four rings of gold, and put the rings on the four corners that are at its four legs. [27] The rings shall be close to the frame, as holders for the poles to bear the table. [28] And you shall make the poles of acacia wood, and overlay them with gold, that the table may be carried with them. [29] You shall make its dishes, its pans, its pitchers, and its bowls for pouring. You shall make them of pure gold. [30] And you shall set the showbread on the table before Me always.

25:31-40

[31] "You shall also make a lampstand of pure gold; the lampstand shall be of hammered work. Its shaft, its branches, its bowls, its ornamental knobs, and flowers shall be of one piece. [32] And six branches shall come out of its sides: three branches of the lampstand out of one side, and three branches of the lampstand out of the other side. [33] Three bowls shall be made like almond blossoms on one branch, with an ornamental knob and a flower, and three bowls made like almond blossoms on the other branch, with an ornamental knob and a flower—and so for the six branches that come out of the lampstand. [34] On the lampstand itself four bowls shall be made like almond blossoms, each with its ornamental knob and flower. [35] And there shall be a knob under the first two branches of the same, a knob under the second two branches of the same, and a knob under the third two branches of the same, according to the six branches that extend from the lampstand.

[36] Their knobs and their branches shall be of one piece; all of it shall be one hammered piece of pure gold. [37] You shall make seven lamps for it, and they shall arrange its lamps so that they give light in front of it. [38] And its wick-trimmers and their trays shall be of pure gold. [39] It shall be made of a talent of pure gold, with all these utensils. [40] And see to it that you make them according to the pattern which was shown you on the mountain.

26:1-6

[1] "Moreover you shall make the tabernacle with ten curtains of fine woven linen and blue, purple and scarlet thread; with artistic designs of cherubim you shall weave them. [2] The length of each curtain shall be twenty-eight cubits, and the width of each curtain four cubits. And every one of the curtains shall have the same measurements. [3] Five curtains shall be coupled to one another, and the other five curtains shall be coupled to one another. [4] And you shall make loops of blue yarn on the edge of the curtain on the selvedge of one set, and likewise you shall do on the outer edge of the other curtain of the second set. [5] Fifty loops you shall make in the one curtain, and fifty loops you shall make on the edge of the curtain that is on the end of the second set, that the loops may be clasped to one another. [6] And you shall make fifty clasps of gold, and couple the curtains together with the clasps, so that it may be one tabernacle.

26:7-14

[7] "You shall also make curtains of goats' hair, to be a tent over the tabernacle. You shall make eleven curtains. [8] The length of each curtain shall be thirty cubits, and the width of each curtain four cubits; and the eleven curtains shall all have the same measurements. [9] And you shall couple five curtains by themselves and six curtains by themselves, and you shall double over the sixth curtain at the forefront of the tent. [10] You shall make fifty loops on the edge of the curtain that is

outermost in one set, and fifty loops on the edge of the curtain of the second set. [11] And you shall make fifty bronze clasps, put the clasps into the loops, and couple the tent together, that it may be one. [12] The remnant that remains of the curtains of the tent, the half curtain that remains, shall hang over the back of the tabernacle. [13] And a cubit on one side and a cubit on the other side, of what remains of the length of the curtains of the tent, shall hang over the sides of the tabernacle, on this side and on that side, to cover it.

[14] "You shall also make a covering of ram skins dyed red for the tent, and a covering of badger skins above that.

26:15-30

[15] "And for the tabernacle you shall make the boards of acacia wood, standing upright. [16] Ten cubits shall be the length of a board, and a cubit and a half shall be the width of each board. [17] Two tenons shall be in each board for binding one to another. Thus you shall make for all the boards of the tabernacle. [18] And you shall make the boards for the tabernacle, twenty boards for the south side. [19] You shall make forty sockets of silver under the twenty boards: two sockets under each of the boards for its two tenons. [20] And for the second side of the tabernacle, the north side, there shall be twenty boards [21] and their forty sockets of silver: two sockets under each of the boards. [22] For the far side of the tabernacle, westward, you shall make six boards. [23] And you shall also make two boards for the two back corners of the tabernacle. [24] They shall be coupled together at the bottom and they shall be coupled together at the top by one ring. Thus it shall be for both of them. They shall be for the two corners. [25] So there shall be eight boards with their sockets of silver—sixteen sockets—two sockets under each of the boards.

[26] "And you shall make bars of acacia wood: five for the boards on one side of the tabernacle, [27] five bars for the boards on the other side of the tabernacle, and five bars for the boards of the side of the tabernacle, for the far side westward. [28] The middle bar shall pass through the midst of the boards from end

to end. ²⁹ You shall overlay the boards with gold, make their rings of gold as holders for the bars, and overlay the bars with gold. ³⁰ And you shall raise up the tabernacle according to its pattern which you were shown on the mountain.

26:31-37

³¹ "You shall make a veil woven of blue, purple and scarlet thread and fine woven linen. It shall be woven with an artistic design of cherubim. ³² You shall hang it upon the four pillars of acacia wood overlaid with gold. Their hooks shall be gold, upon four sockets of silver. ³³ And you shall hang the veil from the clasps. Then you shall bring the ark of the Testimony in there, behind the veil. The veil shall be a divider for you between the holy place and the Most Holy. ³⁴ You shall put the mercy seat upon the ark of the Testimony in the Most Holy. ³⁵ You shall set the table outside the veil, and the lampstand across from the table on the side of the tabernacle toward the south; and you shall put the table on the north side.

³⁶ "You shall make a screen for the door of the tabernacle, woven of blue, purple and scarlet thread and fine woven linen, made by a weaver. ³⁷ And you shall make for the screen five pillars of acacia wood, and overlay them with gold; their hooks shall be gold, and you shall cast five sockets of bronze for them.

27:1-8

¹"You shall make an altar of acacia wood, five cubits long and five cubits wide—the altar shall be square—and its height shall be three cubits. ² You shall make its horns on its four corners; its horns shall be of one piece with it. And you shall overlay it with bronze. ³ Also you shall make its pans to receive its ashes, and its shovels and its basins and its forks and its firepans; you shall make all its utensils of bronze. ⁴ You shall make a grate for it, a network of bronze; and on the network you shall make four bronze rings at its four corners. ⁵ You shall put it under the rim of the altar beneath, that the

network may be midway up the altar. ⁶ And you shall make poles for the altar, poles of acacia wood, and overlay them with bronze. ⁷ The poles shall be put in the rings, and the poles shall be on the two sides of the altar to bear it. ⁸ You shall make it hollow with boards; as it was shown you on the mountain, so shall they make it.

27:9-19

⁹ "You shall also make the court of the tabernacle. For the south side there shall be hangings for the court made of fine woven linen, one hundred cubits long for one side. ¹⁰ And its twenty pillars and their twenty sockets shall be bronze. The hooks of the pillars and their bands shall be silver. ¹¹ Likewise along the length of the north side there shall be hangings one hundred cubits long, with its twenty pillars and their twenty sockets of bronze, and the hooks of the pillars and their bands of silver.

¹² "And along the width of the court on the west side shall be hangings of fifty cubits, with their ten pillars and their ten sockets. ¹³ The width of the court on the east side shall be fifty cubits. ¹⁴ The hangings on one side of the gate shall be fifteen cubits, with their three pillars and their three sockets. ¹⁵ And on the other side shall be hangings of fifteen cubits, with their three pillars and their three sockets.

¹⁶ "For the gate of the court there shall be a screen twenty cubits long, woven of blue, purple and scarlet thread and fine woven linen, made by a weaver. It shall have four pillars and four sockets. ¹⁷ All the pillars around the court shall have bands of silver; their hooks shall be of silver and their sockets of bronze. ¹⁸ The length of the court shall be one hundred cubits, the width fifty throughout, and the height five cubits, made of fine woven linen, and its sockets of bronze. ¹⁹ All the utensils of the tabernacle for all its service, all its pegs, and all the pegs of the court, shall be of bronze."

Ever since the day Moses killed the Egyptian who struck a Hebrew slave and buried him in the sand, thus forcing Moses to flee into the desert, Moses has only had one regret – that he had to leave behind his profession, which was no other than architecture. Moses goes through many trials and tribulations in leading the people through the desert. He finally succeeded in creating God's new image, which he saw as a symbol for uniting the people; an invisible symbol, without shape, a symbol that puts fear into the hearts of those who do not heed the laws that Moses wrote down in order for them to live together in harmony. Moses saw this as the only option for creating unity among the Israelites, and after he succeeds in convincing the people that he's right, that God exists, Moses takes a long vacation, to rest, spend time alone in nature and do what he really loves to do. So as he sits on the mountain all alone, he sets his artistic talents loose and designs the Tabernacle of Meeting as a home for himself and of course a holy place for the people. He knew the job would require a great investment, and so he turns to the people, in God's name, and asks them to donate as much as they can. He then provides a list of items needed to build the holy place. It should be noted that from this point on anyone who came from among the people and wanted to help the Israelites had to open his speeches with 'and the Lord said' or 'then the word of the Lord came to me, saying' all the way until the destruction of the Second Temple. But if someone today even hinted that God spoke to him, even if it were one of the leaders of the world, he would probably be institutionalized immediately.

27:20-21

[20] "And you shall command the children of Israel that they bring you pure oil of pressed olives for the light, to cause the lamp to burn continually. [21] In the tabernacle of meeting, outside the veil which is before the Testimony, Aaron and his sons shall tend it from evening until morning before the LORD. It shall be a statute forever to their generations on behalf of the children of Israel.

28:1-12

¹"Now take Aaron your brother, and his sons with him, from among the children of Israel, that he may minister to Me as priest, Aaron and Aaron's sons: Nadab, Abihu, Eleazar, and Ithamar. ² And you shall make holy garments for Aaron your brother, for glory and for beauty. ³ So you shall speak to all who are gifted artisans, whom I have filled with the spirit of wisdom, that they may make Aaron's garments, to consecrate him, that he may minister to Me as priest. ⁴ And these are the garments which they shall make: a breastplate, an ephod [an ornamented vest], a robe, a skillfully woven tunic, a turban and a sash. So they shall make holy garments for Aaron your brother and his sons, that he may minister to Me as priest.

⁵ "They shall take the gold, blue, purple, and scarlet thread and the fine linen, ⁶ and they shall make the ephod of gold, blue, purple and scarlet thread and fine woven linen, artistically worked. ⁷ It shall have two shoulder straps joined at its two edges, and so it shall be joined together. ⁸ And the intricately woven band of the ephod, which is on it, shall be of the same workmanship, made of gold, blue, purple and scarlet thread and fine woven linen.

⁹ "Then you shall take two onyx stones and engrave on them the names of the sons of Israel: ¹⁰ six of their names on one stone and six names on the other stone, in order of their birth. ¹¹ With the work of an engraver in stone, like the engravings of a signet, you shall engrave the two stones with the names of the sons of Israel. You shall set them in settings of gold. ¹² And you shall put the two stones on the shoulders of the ephod as memorial stones for the sons of Israel. So Aaron shall bear their names before the LORD on his two shoulders as a memorial.

28:13-28

¹³ "You shall also make settings of gold, ¹⁴ and you shall make two chains of pure gold like braided cords, and fasten the braided chains to the settings.

[15] "You shall make the breastplate of judgment. Artistically woven according to the workmanship of the ephod you shall make it: of gold, blue, purple and scarlet thread, and fine woven linen, you shall make it. [16] It shall be doubled into a square: a span shall be its length, and a span shall be its width. [17] And you shall put settings of stones in it, four rows of stones: The first row shall be a sardius, a topaz and an emerald; this shall be the first row; [18] the second row shall be a turquoise, a sapphire and a diamond; [19] the third row, a jacinth, an agate and an amethyst; [20] and the fourth row, a beryl, an onyx and a jasper. They shall be set in gold settings. [21] And the stones shall have the names of the sons of Israel, twelve according to their names, like the engravings of a signet, each one with its own name; they shall be according to the twelve tribes.

[22] "You shall make chains for the breastplate at the end, like braided cords of pure gold. [23] And you shall make two rings of gold for the breastplate, and put the two rings on the two ends of the breastplate. [24] Then you shall put the two braided chains of gold in the two rings which are on the ends of the breastplate; [25] and the other two ends of the two braided chains you shall fasten to the two settings, and put them on the shoulder straps of the ephod in the front.

[26] "You shall make two rings of gold, and put them on the two ends of the breastplate, on the edge of it, which is on the inner side of the ephod. [27] And two other rings of gold you shall make, and put them on the two shoulder straps, underneath the ephod toward its front, right at the seam above the intricately woven band of the ephod. [28] They shall bind the breastplate by means of its rings to the rings of the ephod, using a blue cord, so that it is above the intricately woven band of the ephod, and so that the breastplate does not come loose from the ephod.

28:29-35

[29] "So Aaron shall bear the names of the sons of Israel on the breastplate of judgment over his heart, when he goes into

the holy place, as a memorial before the LORD continually. ³⁰ And you shall put in the breastplate of judgment the Urim and the Thummim, and they shall be over Aaron's heart when he goes in before the LORD. So Aaron shall bear the judgment of the children of Israel over his heart before the LORD continually.

³¹ "You shall make the robe of the ephod all of blue. ³² There shall be an opening for his head in the middle of it; it shall have a woven binding all around its opening, like the opening in a coat of mail, so that it does not tear. ³³ And upon its hem you shall make pomegranates of blue, purple and scarlet, all around its hem, and bells of gold between them all around: ³⁴ a golden bell and a pomegranate, a golden bell and a pomegranate, upon the hem of the robe all around. ³⁵ And it shall be upon Aaron when he ministers, and its sound will be heard when he goes into the holy place before the LORD and when he comes out, that he may not die.

28:36-39

³⁶ "You shall also make a plate of pure gold and engrave on it, like the engraving of a signet:
HOLINESS TO THE LORD.
³⁷ And you shall put it on a blue cord, that it may be on the turban; it shall be on the front of the turban. ³⁸ So it shall be on Aaron's forehead, that Aaron may bear the iniquity of the holy things which the children of Israel hallow in all their holy gifts; and it shall always be on his forehead, that they may be accepted before the LORD.

³⁹ "You shall skillfully weave the tunic of fine linen thread, you shall make the turban of fine linen, and you shall make the sash of woven work.

28:40-43

⁴⁰ "For Aaron's sons you shall make tunics, and you shall make sashes for them. And you shall make hats for them, for glory and beauty. ⁴¹ So you shall put them on Aaron your

brother and on his sons with him. You shall anoint them, consecrate them, and sanctify them, that they may minister to Me as priests. [42] And you shall make for them linen trousers to cover their nakedness; they shall reach from the waist to the thighs. [43] They shall be on Aaron and on his sons when they come into the tabernacle of meeting, or when they come near the altar to minister in the holy place, that they do not incur iniquity and die. It shall be a statute forever to him and his descendants after him."

Now, after Moses finished designing the tabernacle of meeting, he turns his attention to provide for Aaron and his five sons and arranges for them a permanent job in the holy place. Obviously, he does this according to God's specific demands, and, obviously, this work requires special attire. So Moses, a multi-faceted and talented artist, as many architects are, makes time to design unique and exorbitantly expensive clothes for Aaron and his sons, clothes that will suit their new lofty position. All this – Aaron and his sons' position in the holy place, and the design of the clothes – Moses attributes to God's will.

29:1-14

[1] "And this is what you shall do to them to hallow them for ministering to Me as priests: Take one young bull and two rams without blemish, [2] and unleavened bread, unleavened cakes mixed with oil, and unleavened wafers anointed with oil (you shall make them of wheat flour). [3] You shall put them in one basket and bring them in the basket, with the bull and the two rams.

[4] "And Aaron and his sons you shall bring to the door of the tabernacle of meeting, and you shall wash them with water. [5] Then you shall take the garments, put the tunic on Aaron, and the robe of the ephod, the ephod, and the breastplate, and gird him with the intricately woven band of the ephod. [6] You shall put the turban on his head, and put the holy crown on the turban. [7] And you shall take the anointing oil, pour it on his

head, and anoint him. [8] Then you shall bring his sons and put tunics on them. [9] And you shall gird them with sashes, Aaron and his sons, and put the hats on them. The priesthood shall be theirs for a perpetual statute. So you shall consecrate Aaron and his sons.

[10] "You shall also have the bull brought before the tabernacle of meeting, and Aaron and his sons shall put their hands on the head of the bull. [11] Then you shall kill the bull before the LORD, by the door of the tabernacle of meeting. [12] You shall take some of the blood of the bull and put it on the horns of the altar with your finger, and pour all the blood beside the base of the altar. [13] And you shall take all the fat that covers the entrails, the fatty lobe attached to the liver, and the two kidneys and the fat that is on them, and burn them on the altar. [14] But the flesh of the bull, with its skin and its offal, you shall burn with fire outside the camp. It is a sin offering.

29:15-21

[15] "You shall also take one ram, and Aaron and his sons shall put their hands on the head of the ram; [16] and you shall kill the ram, and you shall take its blood and sprinkle it all around on the altar. [17] Then you shall cut the ram in pieces, wash its entrails and its legs, and put them with its pieces and with its head. [18] And you shall burn the whole ram on the altar. It is a burnt offering to the LORD; it is a sweet aroma, an offering made by fire to the LORD.

[19] "You shall also take the other ram, and Aaron and his sons shall put their hands on the head of the ram. [20] Then you shall kill the ram, and take some of its blood and put it on the tip of the right ear of Aaron and on the tip of the right ear of his sons, on the thumb of their right hand and on the big toe of their right foot, and sprinkle the blood all around on the altar. [21] And you shall take some of the blood that is on the altar, and some of the anointing oil, and sprinkle it on Aaron and on his garments, on his sons and on the garments of his sons with him; and he and his garments shall be hallowed, and his sons and his sons' garments with him.

29:22-25

²² "Also you shall take the fat of the ram, the fat tail, the fat that covers the entrails, the fatty lobe attached to the liver, the two kidneys and the fat on them, the right thigh (for it is a ram of consecration),²³ one loaf of bread, one cake made with oil, and one wafer from the basket of the unleavened bread that is before the LORD; ²⁴ and you shall put all these in the hands of Aaron and in the hands of his sons, and you shall wave them as a wave offering before the LORD. ²⁵ You shall receive them back from their hands and burn them on the altar as a burnt offering, as a sweet aroma before the LORD. It is an offering made by fire to the LORD.

29:26

²⁶ "Then you shall take the breast of the ram of Aaron's consecration and wave it as a wave offering before the LORD; and it shall be your portion."

This ceremony, ostensibly guided by God, is meant to ensure that the tastiest parts of the ram are always passed into Moses's hands. The whole ceremony is so simplistic and unnecessary, that it seems to me as though it was performed before people of such low intelligence that they accepted it without hesitation. I find it hard to believe that the majority of people in the world today are still that simple.

29:27-28

²⁷ "And from the ram of the consecration you shall consecrate the breast of the wave offering which is waved, and the thigh of the heave offering which is raised, of that which is for Aaron and of that which is for his sons. ²⁸ It shall be from the children of Israel for Aaron and his sons by a statute forever. For it is a heave offering; it shall be a heave offering

from the children of Israel from the sacrifices of their peace offerings, that is, their heave offering to the LORD.

29:29-35

[29] "And the holy garments of Aaron shall be his sons' after him, to be anointed in them and to be consecrated in them. [30] That son who becomes priest in his place shall put them on for seven days, when he enters the tabernacle of meeting to minister in the holy place.

[31] "And you shall take the ram of the consecration and boil its flesh in the holy place. [32] Then Aaron and his sons shall eat the flesh of the ram, and the bread that is in the basket, by the door of the tabernacle of meeting. [33] They shall eat those things with which the atonement was made, to consecrate and to sanctify them; but an outsider shall not eat them, because they are holy. [34] And if any of the flesh of the consecration offerings, or of the bread, remains until the morning, then you shall burn the remainder with fire. It shall not be eaten, because it is holy.

[35] "<u>Thus you shall do to Aaron and his sons, according to all that I have commanded you. Seven days you shall consecrate them.</u>

29:36-46

[36] "And you shall offer a bull every day as a sin offering for atonement. You shall cleanse the altar when you make atonement for it, and you shall anoint it to sanctify it. [37] Seven days you shall make atonement for the altar and sanctify it. And the altar shall be most holy. Whatever touches the altar must be holy.

[38] "Now this is what you shall offer on the altar: <u>two lambs of the first year, day by day continually.</u> [39] One lamb you shall offer in the morning, and the other lamb you shall offer at twilight. [40] With the one lamb shall be one-tenth of an ephah of flour mixed with one-fourth of a hin of pressed oil, and one-fourth of a hin of wine as a drink offering. [41] And the other

lamb you shall offer at twilight; and you shall offer with it the grain offering and the drink offering, as in the morning, for a sweet aroma, an offering made by fire to the LORD. [42] This shall be a continual burnt offering throughout your generations at the door of the tabernacle of meeting before the LORD, where I will meet you to speak with you. [43] And there I will meet with the children of Israel, and the tabernacle shall be sanctified by My glory. [44] So I will consecrate the tabernacle of meeting and the altar. I will also consecrate both Aaron and his sons to minister to Me as priests. [45] I will dwell among the children of Israel and will be their God. [46] And they shall know that I am the LORD their God, who brought them up out of the land of Egypt, that I may dwell among them. I am the LORD their God."

The underlined verses above explain the commandment, 'Six days you shall work, but on the seventh day you shall rest': that on the Sabbath you mustn't work, but rest, and you can also have fun, and make a fire, and cook. I cannot ignore that man is essentially a herbivore, as every fledgling anthropologist will tell you. It is easy to prove – I have been testing this hypothesis on myself for over twenty years and it is true.

One can also see what happens to cows or chickens when they are given food that is not suitable for them according to the food chain. Perhaps even man turned into a carnivore by eating like a carnivore. So I don't understand why God, who certainly knows all this, would wish Aaron's family to eat meat. And of course, I don't understand why he should care what kind of food his family eats, or any family for that matter. Moses immortalizes the positions of Aaron and his sons through an odd pagan ritual, in order to ensure their easy living. From now on they will never want for clothing or fresh food, the best cuts of meat, and the best and tastiest foods that were known at the time, and all by the order of God of course. It seems to me that in the last chapters Moses develops contempt for the simple people he leads, and more interestingly, seems to enjoy it. As he gained total domination over the people he became a hedonist, though he was probably always like that. He grew up amongst the royal family in Egypt, and the changes he experienced over the past several years made him forget his hedonistic way of life – but it is not hard to return to old habits.

30:11-16

[11] Then the LORD spoke to Moses, saying: [12] "When you take the census of the children of Israel for their number, then every man shall give a ransom for himself to the LORD, when you number them, that there may be no plague among them when you number them. [13] This is what everyone among those who are numbered shall give: half a shekel according to the shekel of the sanctuary (a shekel is twenty gerahs). The half-shekel shall be an offering to the LORD. [14] Everyone included among those who are numbered, from twenty years old and above, shall give an offering to the LORD. [15] The rich shall not give more and the poor shall not give less than half a shekel, when you give an offering to the LORD, to make atonement for yourselves. [16] And you shall take the atonement money of the children of Israel, and shall appoint it for the service of the tabernacle of meeting, that it may be a memorial for the children of Israel before the LORD, to make atonement for yourselves."

After all the expenses Moses had building the tabernacle of meeting, the materials for the expensive clothes for Aaron and his sons, and paying his yes-men at the vision of Mount Sinai, it seems his coffers ran dry. So Moses imposed a head tax in the name of God in order to cover daily expenses for the upkeep of the tabernacle of meeting. You can tell it wasn't really a census, since men under twenty weren't counted, nor women and children – only men over twenty, who then had to pay half a shekel. Which is why the number of people counted was not published, so we don't know how much money went into Moses's coffers.

Genesis 1:27

[27] So God created man in His own image; in the image of God He created him; male and female He created them.

Exodus 3:2-5

[2] And the Angel of the LORD appeared to him in a flame of fire from the midst of a bush. So he looked, and behold, the bush was burning with fire, but the bush was not consumed. [3] Then Moses said, "I will now turn aside and see this great sight, why the bush does not burn."
[4] So when the LORD saw that he turned aside to look, God called to him from the midst of the bush and said, "Moses, Moses!"
And he said, "Here I am."
[5] Then He said, "Do not draw near this place. Take your sandals off your feet, for the place where you stand is holy ground."

Exodus 16:10

[10] Now it came to pass, as Aaron spoke to the whole congregation of the children of Israel, that they looked toward the wilderness, and behold, the glory of the LORD appeared in the cloud.

Exodus 19:16-21

[16] Then it came to pass on the third day, in the morning, that there were thunderings and lightnings, and a thick cloud on the mountain; and the sound of the trumpet was very loud, so that all the people who were in the camp trembled. [17] And Moses brought the people out of the camp to meet with God, and they stood at the foot of the mountain. [18] Now Mount Sinai was completely in smoke, because the LORD descended upon it in fire. Its smoke ascended like the smoke of a furnace, and the whole mountain quaked greatly. [19] And when the blast of the

trumpet sounded long and became louder and louder, Moses spoke, and God answered him by voice. [20] Then the LORD came down upon Mount Sinai, on the top of the mountain. And the LORD called Moses to the top of the mountain, and Moses went up.

[21] And the LORD said to Moses, "Go down and warn the people, lest they break through to gaze at the LORD, and many of them perish.

Exodus 20:21

[21] So the people stood afar off, but Moses drew near the thick darkness where God was.

Exodus 20:22

[22] Then the LORD said to Moses, "Thus you shall say to the children of Israel: 'You have seen that I have talked with you from heaven'."

Exodus 24:9-11

[9] Then Moses went up, also Aaron, Nadab, and Abihu, and seventy of the elders of Israel, [10] and they saw the God of Israel. And there was under His feet as it were a paved work of sapphire stone, and it was like the very heavens in its clarity. [11] But on the nobles of the children of Israel He did not lay His hand. So they saw God, and they ate and drank.

Exodus 24:17-18

[17] The sight of the glory of the LORD was like a consuming fire on the top of the mountain in the eyes of the children of Israel. [18] So Moses went into the midst of the cloud and went up into the mountain.

Exodus 25:8-11

⁸ And let them make Me a sanctuary, that I may dwell among them. ⁹ According to all that I show you, that is, the pattern of the tabernacle and the pattern of all its furnishings, just so you shall make it.
¹⁰ "And they shall make an ark of acacia wood; two and a half cubits shall be its length, a cubit and a half its width, and a cubit and a half its height. ¹¹ And you shall overlay it with pure gold, inside and out you shall overlay it, and shall make on it a molding of gold all around."

The quotes above are a choice selection of the forms God takes. Moses knew that many of the Israelites did not believe in the god Jehovah at all. They were used to believing in something they could be close to, something they could see, hold, maybe even kiss – especially in times of need when one needed someone to pour one's heart to, even if it was just a small statue. Moses came to understand this only after all his attempts at creating a great, scary, dangerous god who could perhaps only scare a certain type of person, but not the slaves who left Egypt. By the time he understood this, it was too late. All the sights and visions he created thinking the people were simple and dumb did not produce the results he had hoped for. To this day we see that every faith and religion has a statue, picture or some sort of small idols that are held dear. This is also true of the three main monotheistic faiths that believe in the Lord God. Moses's undoing was the sudden spate of extravagance that came over him, in addition to his concern for Aaron and his sons. It seems that not everyone was as simple as Moses supposed.

30:17-21

¹⁷ Then the LORD spoke to Moses, saying: ¹⁸ "You shall also make a laver of bronze, with its base also of bronze, for washing. You shall put it between the tabernacle of meeting and the altar. And you shall put water in it, ¹⁹ for Aaron and his

sons shall wash their hands and their feet in water from it. [20] When they go into the tabernacle of meeting, or when they come near the altar to minister, to burn an offering made by fire to the LORD, they shall wash with water, lest they die. [21] So they shall wash their hands and their feet, lest they die. And it shall be a statute forever to them—to him and his descendants throughout their generations."

Moses continues to invest in the tabernacle of meeting, and various items that will make Aaron and his sons comfortable. However, I don't understand why anyone entering the tabernacle of meeting must wash their hands and feet or die; it seems Moses decides to enforce belief in God the hard way.

31:12-18

[12] And the LORD spoke to Moses, saying, [13] "Speak also to the children of Israel, saying: 'Surely My Sabbaths you shall keep, for it is a sign between Me and you throughout your generations, that you may know that I am the LORD who sanctifies you. [14] You shall keep the Sabbath, therefore, for it is holy to you. Everyone who profanes it shall surely be put to death; for whoever does any work on it, that person shall be cut off from among his people. [15] Work shall be done for six days, but the seventh is the Sabbath of rest, holy to the LORD. Whoever does any work on the Sabbath day, he shall surely be put to death. [16] Therefore the children of Israel shall keep the Sabbath, to observe the Sabbath throughout their generations as a perpetual covenant. [17] It is a sign between Me and the children of Israel forever; for in six days the LORD made the heavens and the earth, and on the seventh day He rested and was refreshed.'"

[18] And when He had made an end of speaking with him on Mount Sinai, He gave Moses two tablets of the Testimony, tablets of stone, written with the finger of God.

I don't see why Moses felt the need to punish those who do not keep the Sabbath so harshly with a death sentence. It stands out since he did not increase the severity of punishment for any of the other commandments, though breaking any one of them is a much worse offense. Even so, Moses changes verse 20:11 ' For in six days the LORD made the heavens and the earth, the sea, and all that is in them, <u>and rested the seventh day.</u>' to 31:17 '... for in six days the LORD made the heavens and the earth, and on the seventh day <u>He rested and was refreshed</u>.' From these verses it is clear that it is permissible to go on vacation, or light a fire, and cook meat, as we have already seen in 29:38 '<u>Now this is what you shall offer on the altar: two lambs of the first year, day by day continually.</u>' – including Saturdays of course.

32:1-6

[1] Now when the people saw that Moses delayed coming down from the mountain, the people gathered together to Aaron, and said to him, "Come, make us gods that shall go before us; for as for this Moses, the man who brought us up out of the land of Egypt, we do not know what has become of him."

[2] And Aaron said to them, "Break off the golden earrings which are in the ears of your wives, your sons, and your daughters, and bring them to me." [3] So all the people broke off the golden earrings which were in their ears, and brought them to Aaron. [4] And he received the gold from their hand, and he fashioned it with an engraving tool, and made a molded calf.

Then they said, "This is your god, O Israel, that brought you out of the land of Egypt!"

[5] So when Aaron saw it, he built an altar before it. And Aaron made a proclamation and said, "Tomorrow is a feast to the LORD." [6] Then they rose early on the next day, offered burnt offerings, and brought peace offerings; and the people sat down to eat and drink, and rose up to play.

Since Moses keeps spending money making himself and his family comfortable, he's suddenly caught in a bit of a jam – he no longer has the resources to maintain his private army or support Aaron and his sons. So Moses and his brother Aaron come up with a scheme to get hold of whatever gold remained after the Israelites made their donations and paid their taxes. And who else would be in charge of this performance other than Aaron himself? But first, why would the people gather around Aaron? Why were the people so desperate for a god, or for Moses's replacement who had made himself almost as a god before them? After all, Moses had been gone for longer periods of time before (for example, when he went up the mountain to meet God and design the tabernacle of meeting) and nothing out of the ordinary happened in his absence then.

Most importantly, Aaron makes no attempt to calm the people. It is he, who despite having seen God on a number of occasions, turns to the people and orders them to give away all of their gold and wastes no time creating the gold idol. What is most astounding about this incident, is that it proves that the Israelites did not believe in the Lord God at all, and were quite willing to do without Moses. The ease with which Aaron's request was accepted, that they give away their gold to create a new god, shows that the people wanted change and that Moses was a dictator who ruled with an iron fist.

32:7-13

[7] And the LORD said to Moses, "Go, get down! For your people whom you brought out of the land of Egypt have corrupted themselves. [8] They have turned aside quickly out of the way which I commanded them. They have made themselves a molded calf, and worshiped it and sacrificed to it, and said, 'This is your god, O Israel, that brought you out of the land of Egypt!'" [9] And the LORD said to Moses, "I have seen this people, and indeed it is a stiff-necked people! [10] Now therefore, let Me alone, that My wrath may burn hot against them and I may consume them. And I will make of you a great nation."

[11] Then Moses pleaded with the LORD his God, and said: "LORD, why does Your wrath burn hot against Your people whom You have brought out of the land of Egypt with great

power and with a mighty hand? [12] Why should the Egyptians speak, and say, 'He brought them out to harm them, to kill them in the mountains, and to consume them from the face of the earth?' Turn from Your fierce wrath, and relent from this harm to Your people. [13] Remember Abraham, Isaac, and Israel, Your servants, to whom You swore by Your own self, and said to them, 'I will multiply your descendants as the stars of heaven; and all this land that I have spoken of I give to your descendants, and they shall inherit it forever.'"

Once again, God decides to wipe out the Jewish people and at the same time promises to make Moses into a great nation. But Moses manages to mollify God by reciting parts of that old mantra promising the land to the descendants of Abraham, Isaac and, Israel (since this occurred after Jacob's name was changed).

33:1

Then the LORD said to Moses, "Depart and go up from here, you and the people whom you have brought out of the land of Egypt, to the land of which I swore to Abraham, Isaac, and Jacob, saying, 'To your descendants I will give it.'"

As it turns out, God himself forgets that he changed Jacob's name to Israel.

32:15-20

[15] And Moses turned and went down from the mountain, and the two tablets of the Testimony were in his hand. The tablets were written on both sides; on the one side and on the other they were written. [16] Now the tablets were the work of God, and the writing was the writing of God engraved on the tablets.
[17] And when Joshua heard the noise of the people as they shouted, he said to Moses, "There is a noise of war in the camp."

¹⁸ But he said: "It is not the noise of the shout of victory, nor the noise of the cry of defeat, but the sound of singing I hear."

¹⁹ So it was, as soon as he came near the camp, that he saw the calf and the dancing. So Moses's anger became hot, and he cast the tablets out of his hands and broke them at the foot of the mountain. ²⁰ Then he took the calf which they had made, burned it in the fire, and ground it to powder; and he scattered it on the water and made the children of Israel drink it.

Moses descends from the mountain with the tablets of the Testimony, which he chiselled carefully for forty days, and sees the people dancing around the golden idol. He immediately smashes the tablets on a rock and proceeds to melt down the golden calf. Masonry and sculpture must have been required classes for architecture students in Egypt. Ostensibly if Moses broke the tablets of the Testimony, then he offended the Lord; no artist wants his work to be treated that way. But do not worry, the tablets were not written by God – clear and simple. God created the world and everything written in Genesis in six days, merely by thinking, so it is quite impossible that the Lord would spend forty days preparing the tablets of the Testimony; it is an incredible insult to God. Only a tired old mason who hasn't practiced the skill since school would take forty days to create the tablets of the Testimony.

32:21-29

²¹ And Moses said to Aaron, "What did this people do to you that you have brought so great a sin upon them?"

²² So Aaron said, "Do not let the anger of my lord become hot. You know the people, that they are set on evil. ²³ For they said to me, 'Make us gods that shall go before us; as for this Moses, the man who brought us out of the land of Egypt, we do not know what has become of him.' ²⁴ And I said to them, 'Whoever has any gold, let them break it off.' So they gave it to me, and I cast it into the fire, and this calf came out."

^{25} Now when Moses saw that the people were unrestrained (for Aaron had not restrained them, to their shame among their enemies), ^{26} then Moses stood in the entrance of the camp, and said, "Whoever is on the LORD's side—come to me!" And all the sons of Levi gathered themselves together to him. ^{27} And he said to them, "Thus says the LORD God of Israel: 'Let every man put his sword on his side, and go in and out from entrance to entrance throughout the camp, and let every man kill his brother, every man his companion, and every man his neighbor.'" ^{28} So the sons of Levi did according to the word of Moses. And about three thousand men of the people fell that day. ^{29} Then Moses said, "Consecrate yourselves today to the LORD that He may bestow on you a blessing this day, for every man has opposed his son and his brother."

Moses plays dumb and accuses his brother Aaron with the question, 'What did this people do to you that you have brought so great a sin upon them?' The whole conversation between Moses and Aaron sounds like a bad play, I dare say even a comedy. But then Moses gives his army the signal. Using the Lord's name as justification for mass murder of his people, who supposedly worshipped the golden calf, he orders his army to kill their own brethren. On this day three thousand innocent people are murdered in cold blood, the recently received commandment 'You shall not kill', ink still wet, as it were, disregarded. All this simply because Moses realized that the people were happy to let him go. He wanted to take back full control of the Israelites even if the price involved was killing some of them. Obviously, the survivors were overcome by fear, and they surrendered to Moses and his army. Moses and his army slaughtered 3,000 people, allegedly because they worshiped the golden calf. But I would not be surprised if a list is uncovered with the names of marked men, possibly those who would not pay taxes, or planned to overthrow Moses, proving that this whole operation was planned in advance.

32:30-35

30 Now it came to pass on the next day that Moses said to the people, "You have committed a great sin. So now I will go up to the LORD; perhaps I can make atonement for your sin." **31** Then Moses returned to the LORD and said, "Oh, these people have committed a great sin, and have made for themselves a god of gold! **32** Yet now, if You will forgive their sin—but if not, I pray, blot me out of Your book which You have written."

33 And the LORD said to Moses, "Whoever has sinned against Me, I will blot him out of My book. **34** Now therefore, go, lead the people to the place of which I have spoken to you. Behold, My Angel shall go before you. Nevertheless, in the day when I visit for punishment, I will visit punishment upon them for their sin."

35 So the LORD plagued the people because of what they did with the calf which Aaron made.

It can no longer be disputed that Moses liked to torment stupid people; after this horrendous massacre Moses tells the people that he is going back up the mountain to try and atone for their sins and ask God for forgiveness. How odd – Moses, who together with his army slaughtered three thousand people, feigns innocence and goes to convince God to forgive the people for the fact that they were innocent victims of a massacre. I remind you again that there are thousands of religions and faiths on this planet, so one cannot simply slaughter those who think differently, especially with regards to religious faith.

33:7-11

7 Moses took his tent and pitched it outside the camp, far from the camp, and called it the tabernacle of meeting. And it came to pass that everyone who sought the LORD went out to the tabernacle of meeting which was outside the camp. **8** So it was, whenever Moses went out to the tabernacle, that all the people rose, and each man stood at his tent door and watched Moses until he had gone into the tabernacle. [9] And it came to pass, when Moses entered the tabernacle, that the pillar of cloud descended and stood at the door of the tabernacle, and the LORD talked with Moses. [10] All the people saw the pillar of cloud standing at the tabernacle door, and all the people rose and worshiped, each man in his tent door. [11] So the LORD spoke to Moses face to face, as a man speaks to his friend. And he would return to the camp

After the massacre, Moses understood that for security reasons he could not continue to reside within the camp, despite having a private army. So Moses moves the tabernacle of meeting outside the camp – far outside the camp. Perhaps Moses even understood that he could not continue in his extreme ways, killing anyone who did not obey his wishes. But a man like Moses does not easily give up everything he had built and created since leaving Egypt, so he manufactures a visit by God himself at the entrance of the tabernacle so that people will see and know God exists and is looking out for Moses.

34:11-17

[11] "Observe what I command you this day. Behold, I am driving out from before you the Amorite and the Canaanite and the Hittite and the Perizzite and the Hivite and the Jebusite. [12] Take heed to yourself, lest you make a covenant with the inhabitants of the land where you are going, lest it be a snare in your midst. [13] But you shall destroy their altars, break their sacred pillars, and cut down their wooden images [14] (for you shall worship no other god, for the LORD, whose name is Jealous, is a jealous God), [15] lest you make a covenant with the inhabitants of the land, and they play the harlot with their gods and make sacrifice to their gods, and one of them invites you and you eat of his sacrifice, [16] and you take of his daughters for your sons, and his daughters play the harlot with their gods and make your sons play the harlot with their gods.

¹⁷ "You shall make no molded gods for yourselves."

Flouting this ban on creating alliances with the inhabitants of the land was probably the downfall of former prime minister Yitzhak Rabin, and the reason he was destined to die.

34:24-26

²⁴ "For I will cast out the nations before you and enlarge your borders; neither will any man covet your land when you go up to appear before the LORD your God three times in the year.
²⁵ "You shall not offer the blood of My sacrifice with leaven, nor shall the sacrifice of the Feast of the Passover be left until morning.
²⁶ "The first of the first fruits of your land you shall bring to the house of the LORD your God. You shall not boil a young goat in its mother's milk."

"You shall not boil a young goat in its mother's milk" is mentioned again as a humane tenet. More and more it seems that the Lord God was made of flesh and blood who resembled man, rather than the other way round, as it stated in Genesis 'in the image of God He created him'. All this we can deduce from the amount of food he orders from his followers at every opportunity. Imagine to yourself that the Israelites who followed Moses in the desert, and numbered over a million people, each gave the Lord a tenth of their crops – that is a tremendous amount of food. Or perhaps those ordering the food for God were those working in the holy place and only they and their families enjoyed these quantities of food.

In addition, it turns out that the Lord had a book that lists all the people on the earth. We find out about this when Moses asks the Lord: (32:32-33) 'Yet now, if You will forgive their sin—but if not, I pray, blot me out of Your book which You have written.' And the LORD said to Moses, 'Whoever has sinned against Me, I will blot him out of My book.' And this is precisely the kind of book that Moses had. A book where he wrote down the names of all the people who opposed him or plotted against him.

34:27-35

[27] Then the LORD said to Moses, "Write these words, for according to the tenor of these words I have made a covenant with you and with Israel." [28] So he was there with the LORD forty days and forty nights; he neither ate bread nor drank water. And He wrote on the tablets the words of the covenant, the Ten Commandments.
[29] Now it was so, when Moses came down from Mount Sinai (and the two tablets of the Testimony were in Moses's hand when he came down from the mountain), that Moses did not know that the skin of his face shone while he talked with Him. [30] So when Aaron and all the children of Israel saw Moses, behold, the skin of his face shone, and they were afraid to come near him. [31] Then Moses called to them, and Aaron and all the rulers of the congregation returned to him; and Moses talked with them. [32] Afterward all the children of Israel came near, and he gave them as commandments all that the LORD had spoken with him on Mount Sinai. [33] And when Moses had finished speaking with them, he put a veil on his face. [34] But whenever Moses went in before the LORD to speak with Him, he would take the veil off until he came out; and he would come out and speak to the children of Israel whatever he had been commanded. [35] And whenever the children of Israel saw the face of Moses, that the skin of Moses's face shone, then Moses would put the veil on his face again, until he went in to speak with Him.

Here we see that the Lord tasks Moses with writing the second set of tablets of Testimony, and also that it took Moses, as a mason, forty days to chisel the tablets.
Before Moses comes down from the mountain he applies to his face the same substance he used when he practiced his first performance in front of Pharaoh: (4:6-7) `Furthermore the LORD said to him, "Now put your hand in your bosom." And

he put his hand in his bosom, and when he took it out, behold, his hand was leprous, like snow. And He said, "Put your hand in your bosom again." So he put his hand in his bosom again, and drew it out of his bosom, and behold, it was restored like his other flesh.' This is the third time that Moses uses this cream or secret powder. The second time he used was in Exodus 24:9-10 'Then Moses went up, also Aaron, Nadab, and Abihu, and seventy of the elders of Israel, and they saw the God of Israel. And there was under His feet as it were a paved work of sapphire stone, and it was like the very heavens in its clarity.' An important detail I noticed, is that it seems Moses stopped stuttering. It seems the desert air was good for him and ever since he is able to speak freely, especially with God.

35:1-3

[1] Then Moses gathered all the congregation of the children of Israel together, and said to them, "These are the words which the LORD has commanded you to do: [2] Work shall be done for six days, but the seventh day shall be a holy day for you, a Sabbath of rest to the LORD. Whoever does any work on it shall be put to death. [3] You shall kindle no fire throughout your dwellings on the Sabbath day."

Anyone who does work on Saturday (the Sabbath) and any who makes a fire on Saturday will be put to death! Work on a Saturday is not really an offense at all. After all, almost all the inhabitants of this planet work regularly or occasionally on Saturday. Think for a moment, should all the citizens of Earth really be put to death? Moses must have a reason for making such a harsh decision in the name of the Lord. Not to mention that the Lord's focused interest in such a small people makes him a local, pagan god.

An overview of Genesis and Exodus reveals that God created the world and all that lives and grows upon it, including man, and that among all the people who populated it (and an explanation for that is still needed) God chose the descendants of Abraham, Isaac and Jacob as his chosen people.

But he never explains why. God sends his chosen, Moses, to liberate and free the chosen people who were slaves in Egypt and promises Moses the land of Canaan forever. Canaan was populated by six other nations that were also created by God, but for some reason they were sentenced to be stricken from the earth. We do not know if, or how, they did evil in the eye of the Lord, but unlike them the chosen people have not stopped doing evil in his eyes to this day; it is mentioned in almost every book of the Bible which tells the history of the Jewish people until the end of the Age of Kings.

Around that time, more or less, a messiah appears in Nazareth, who was God's son according to the Christian faith. Then the real troubles begin for the chosen people, a difficult time, a time of unbearable hardships, robbery, theft, exploitation, humiliation, baseless blood libel, and every possible attempt at annihilating the Jews.

In his book *World History of the Jewish People*, author Simon Dubnow chronicles the history of the Jewish people from its very beginning and until the rise of the Nazis in Germany. In my opinion, this is one of the best books, or even the best book ever written about the history of the Jewish people. If any of you consider reading this masterpiece (it's ten volumes or so), make sure to have a box of tissues at hand, even if you think yourself a fairly tough person. As a man of faith I understand that all this suffering was because the chosen people strayed and did not follow God's will. But after two thousand years of suffering and exile all over the world the Lord decides once again to annihilate the chosen people! Strike them from his book! (32:33) 'Whoever has sinned against Me, I will blot him out of My book.' For this reason God chose a simple man, a man from among the most educated nation of that period. This man spent his time in the cellars of his country's capital, and from there he managed to excite the people. As I mentioned, this was a most developed nation: intellectually, technologically and in terms of literature and culture a nation blessed with the best composers who created exquisite symphonies which have not been equalled to this day. The man convinced the people of such a nation to annihilate the chosen people! And of course most of the German people helped. But, like they say, the Lord works in mysterious ways. In the last minute God decided 'No more!' and the killing stopped.

We'll end with the biggest phenomenon since creation. Abraham in his delusions invents God. After him Moses, the multi-talented artist, adopts the idea and takes it to new heights, wishing to become a supreme god himself. He does not succeed and so compromises and remains God's messenger on earth. Crowning Moses's doctrine is the concept that no one could see God without dying immediately, and after all no one wishes to die. And so the Lord became a supreme god, without anyone seeing him or wanting to see him, despite the fact that he has never given anyone a sign of his existence. But I know of a tragic event that took place in France in 1429 when the English ruled France. A young peasant girl by the name of Joan of Arc, without any military background, claimed that she received a message from God and was thus able to unite the French people and lead them to war against the English and liberate France. The Church would not accept her presenting herself as having had a divine revelation, and did everything in its power to capture and burn her as a witch. The court of the inquisition gave her the option to repent and say she did not receive a message from God and thus save her life, but she refused and was burned alive at the stake. Centuries later the church canonized her a saint. Why did the church not believe her? Did they know the truth even then?

Leviticus

1:1-9

[1] Now the Lord called to Moses, and spoke to him from the tabernacle of meeting, saying, [2] "Speak to the children of Israel, and say to them: 'When any one of you brings an offering to the Lord, you shall bring your offering of the livestock—of the herd and of the flock.'

[3] "If his offering is a burnt sacrifice of the herd, let him offer a male without blemish; he shall offer it of his own free will at the door of the tabernacle of meeting before the Lord. [4] Then he shall put his hand on the head of the burnt offering, and it will be accepted on his behalf to make atonement for him. [5] He shall kill the bull before the Lord; and the priests, Aaron's sons, shall bring the blood and sprinkle the blood all around on the altar that is by the door of the tabernacle of meeting. [6] And he shall skin the burnt offering and cut it into its pieces. [7] The sons of Aaron the priest shall put fire on the altar, and lay the wood in order on the fire. [8] Then the priests, Aaron's sons, shall lay the parts, the head, and the fat in order on the wood that is on the fire upon the altar; [9] but he shall wash its entrails and its legs with water. And the priest shall burn all on the altar as a burnt sacrifice, an offering made by fire, a sweet aroma to the Lord."

Were I not certain that these were the Lord's words to Moses, I would think that this is a rancher's convention in some South American country where they meet to exchange stories about treating and eating meat.

The first chapters in Leviticus are dedicated to the way God loves his meat sacrificed. Not simply another sheep, or cow or young goat; the meat must be rinsed and cleaned, taken apart into cuts and seasoned with salt. One could also serve pigeons, or various baked goods of course.

A judicial system was established in which God directed Moses in his role as judge, and the sentences often involved sacrificing meat to God. One might get the impression that God turned hedonistic and loves the smell of meat and gourmet food. God's preoccupation with meat certainly mars his image, at least in my opinion, and I would go so far as to say that it calls into question his very existence. The strong contrast between the creation of the world and the descent, or perhaps more appropriately, the fall, the deterioration into an abyss of preoccupation with meats, obviously casts serious doubts on God's very existence.

2:4-13

[4] "And if you bring as an offering, a grain offering baked in the oven, it shall be unleavened cakes of fine flour mixed with oil, or unleavened wafers anointed with oil. [5] But if your offering is a grain offering baked in a pan, it shall be of fine flour, unleavened, mixed with oil. [6] You shall break it in pieces and pour oil on it; it is a grain offering.

[7] "If your offering is a grain offering baked in a covered pan, it shall be made of fine flour with oil. [8] You shall bring the grain offering that is made of these things to the Lord. And when it is presented to the priest, he shall bring it to the altar. [9] Then the priest shall take from the grain offering a memorial portion, and burn it on the altar. It is an offering made by fire, a sweet aroma to the Lord. [10] And what is left of the grain offering shall be Aaron's and his sons'. It is most holy of the offerings to the Lord made by fire.

[11] "No grain offering which you bring to the Lord shall be made with leaven, for you shall burn no leaven nor any honey in any offering to the Lord made by fire. [12] As for the offering of the first fruits, you shall offer them to the Lord, but they shall not be burned on the altar for a sweet aroma. [13] And every offering of your grain offering you shall season with salt; you shall not allow the salt of the covenant of your God to be lacking from your grain offering. With all your offerings you shall offer salt.

6:14-17

[14] "This is the law of the grain offering: The sons of Aaron shall offer it on the altar before the Lord. [15] He shall take from it his handful of the fine flour of the grain offering, with its oil, and all the frankincense which is on the grain offering, and shall burn it on the altar for a sweet aroma, as a memorial to the Lord. [16] And the remainder of it Aaron and his sons shall eat; with unleavened bread it shall be eaten in a holy place; in the court of the tabernacle of meeting they shall eat it. [17] It shall not be baked with leaven. I have given it as their portion of My offerings made by fire; … Everyone who touches them must be holy."

7:28-36

[28] Then the Lord spoke to Moses, saying, [29] "Speak to the children of Israel, saying: 'He who offers the sacrifice of his peace offering to the Lord shall bring his offering to the Lord from the sacrifice of his peace offering. [30] His own hands shall bring the offerings made by fire to the Lord. The fat with the breast he shall bring, that the breast may be waved as a wave offering before the Lord. [31] And the priest shall burn the fat on the altar, but the breast shall be Aaron's and his sons'. [32] Also the right thigh you shall give to the priest as a heave offering from the sacrifices of your peace offerings. [33] He among the sons of Aaron, who offers the blood of the peace offering and the fat, shall have the right thigh for his part. [34] For the breast of the wave offering and the thigh of the heave offering I have taken from the children of Israel, from the sacrifices of their peace offerings, and I have given them to Aaron the priest and to his sons from the children of Israel by a statute forever.'"

[35] This is the consecrated portion for Aaron and his sons, from the offerings made by fire to the Lord, on the day when Moses presented them to minister to the Lord as priests. [36] The Lord commanded this to be given to them by the children of

Israel, on the day that He anointed them, by a statute forever throughout their generations.

Once again we witness a simple pagan ritual where God ostensibly decides who gets the best cut of each sacrifice burned in his name. In fact, all religions and faiths are based on pagan rites; the rituals provide the masses with meaning to their lives. 'Religion is the opiate of the masses' says it all. The rituals usually take place during each faith's holidays and are mostly geared towards children thus taking hold in their consciousness, so eventually the children identify with the group. When these children grow up, some will study and acquire an education and a wide general knowledge; as they go on with their lives, these ceremonies will become merely tradition. Others will grow up full of messianic thoughts and can be very dangerous to themselves, and more importantly to the whole world. We need only remember all the victims, the people slaughtered by the three monotheistic faiths despite their commandment of 'Thou shalt not kill'! The paradox is that all the murderers claim to be part of God's army and the murder continues unabated to this day, and probably will continue for many years. A main factor in the continuation of such violence in the future is that extremist sects will gradually take control of governments in many countries. They will do this by exploiting the greed of elected officials, or through the masses who are looking for apocalyptic change, which for convenience we will call a higher power. All this, of course, while suppressing rational general education in favor of religious studies – each according to its faith, and I remind you again that there are thousands of sects and faiths across this globe!

10:1-7

[1] Then Nadab and Abihu, the sons of Aaron, each took his censer and put fire in it, put incense on it, and offered profane fire before the Lord, which He had not commanded them. [2] So fire went out from the Lord and devoured them, and they died

before the Lord. ³ And Moses said to Aaron, "This is what the Lord spoke, saying: 'By those who come near Me I must be regarded as holy; and before all the people I must be glorified.'" So Aaron held his peace.

⁴ Then Moses called Mishael and Elzaphan, the sons of Uzziel the uncle of Aaron, and said to them, "Come near, carry your brethren from before the sanctuary out of the camp." ⁵ So they went near and carried them by their tunics out of the camp, as Moses had said.

⁶ And Moses said to Aaron, and to Eleazar and Ithamar, his sons, "Do not uncover your heads nor tear your clothes, lest you die, and wrath come upon all the people. But let your brethren, the whole house of Israel, bewail the burning which the Lord has kindled. **7** You shall not go out from the door of the tabernacle of meeting, lest you die, for the anointing oil of the Lord is upon you." And they did according to the word of Moses.

10:8-11

⁸ Then the Lord spoke to Aaron, saying: ⁹ "Do not drink wine or intoxicating drink, you, nor your sons with you, when you go into the tabernacle of meeting, lest you die. It shall be a statute forever throughout your generations, ¹⁰ that you may distinguish between holy and unholy, and between unclean and clean, ¹¹ and that you may teach the children of Israel all the statutes which the Lord has spoken to them by the hand of Moses."

From the beginning of Leviticus we witness the formation of a group of people whose entire duty is to serve in the holy place. These people are responsible for all the foods given in the tabernacle of meeting as sacrifice for the Lord. Moses passes along God's will to the people, especially what kinds of foods are suitable for His table, and how to treat the various meats according to God's requests. But then a horrible accident takes place and two of Aaron's sons, who were sanctified by God to serve in the holy place, are burned alive because they used profane fire. We were aware that they were in charge of sacrifices, but profane fire is a new, unfamiliar term used to explain why God incinerated two of Aaron's sons whom he himself had chosen to serve him. Though the use of profane fire may have been a grave offense, there was room for compassion and forgiveness, after all the Lord is 'merciful and gracious, longsuffering, and abounding in goodness and truth, [7] keeping mercy for thousands, forgiving iniquity and transgression and sin' (Exodus 34:6).

From an exhaustive investigation I have made into this incident it turns out that the fire broke out when the two sons' clothes caught fire, as they had previously been anointed with oil. The fire broke out when they were busy with their holy work and so were not careful to keep their distance from the fire. Judging by the number of empty bottles I found strewn in the tent I concluded that the victims were intoxicated. I also noticed there were no warning signs, fire extinguishers or any other fire safety equipment. As a result I have recommended that alcoholic beverages should not be consumed in the tabernacle of meeting, especially during holy work.

Reading Leviticus makes it clear beyond a doubt that man created God. God created the universe and all that is in it in six days merely with his words; there is no doubt that God is a higher intelligence even an ultimate being! Simply speaking, it is not possible that from such heights God would descend so low as to require pagan meat rituals that are intended for those of low intelligence. It does not befit the God who created the world in six days. Moreover, the group that worked in the holy place positioned itself as a highly privileged class. It was while reading Leviticus that the famous Spanish philosopher, who preferred to remain anonymous in this instance, coined the phrase 'El vivo vive del sonso y el sonso vive de su trabajo', or in English: 'The wise live off the dumb, and the dumb live off their work'.

17:1-4

¹And the Lord spoke to Moses, saying, ² "Speak to Aaron, to his sons, and to all the children of Israel, and say to them, 'This is the thing which the Lord has commanded, saying: ³ "Whatever man of the house of Israel who kills an ox or lamb or goat in the camp, or who kills it outside the camp, ⁴ and does not bring it to the door of the tabernacle of meeting to offer an offering to the Lord before the tabernacle of the Lord, the guilt of bloodshed shall be imputed to that man. He has shed blood; *and that man shall be cut off from among his people .*"'

Any of the House of Israel who slaughters an ox, sheep, or goat in or outside the camp and does not bring it to the tabernacle to give sacrifice shall be put to death! This is the meaning of the verb "cut off" as it is used in the Hebrew Bible, whereas in the English translations the verb used means excommunication; which, in primitive tribal contexts, is often as bad as death, to all intents and purposes.

17:8

⁸ "Also you shall say to them: 'Whatever man of the house of Israel, or of the strangers who dwell among you, who offers a burnt offering or sacrifice, ⁹ and does not bring it to the door of the tabernacle of meeting, to offer it to the Lord, *that man shall be cut off from among his people.*'"

This is the second time that this law appears, immediately after the first. Every man from the house of Israel, including strangers who live among them (so they do not use the strangers as a *Shabbos goy* or 'workaround'), who cooks meat on the fire and does not bring the meat to the tabernacle of meeting must be killed! This seems rather extreme. It seems that the people did not want to feed Moses' private army and those working in the holy place, so a draconic law was enacted. Obviously no one refused, since they remembered the massacre of 3,000 innocent people in cold blood, which is what happened the last time they defied him.

17:10

¹⁰ "And whatever man of the house of Israel, or of the strangers who dwell among you, who eats any blood, I will set My face against that person who eats blood, *and will cut him off from among his people.*"

Any man of the house of Israel who eats blood sausage, or any meat with blood in it, without salting it first incurs an automatic death sentence and shall be exterminated!

17:11-14

¹¹ "For the life of the flesh is in the blood, and I have given it to you upon the altar to make atonement for your souls; for it is the blood that makes atonement for the soul. ¹² Therefore I said to the children of Israel, 'No one among you shall eat blood, nor shall any stranger who dwells among you eat blood'."
¹³ "Whatever man of the children of Israel, or of the strangers who dwell among you, who hunts and catches any animal or bird that may be eaten, he shall pour out its blood and cover it with dust; ¹⁴ for it is the life of all flesh. Its blood sustains its life. Therefore I said to the children of Israel, 'You shall not eat the blood of any flesh, for the life of all flesh is its blood. *Whoever eats it shall be cut of*'"

The ban on eating an animal's blood is mentioned a second time, and the punishment for anyone who breaks this law is death.

18:22-29

²² "You shall not lie with a male as with a woman. It is an abomination. ²³ Nor shall you mate with any animal, to defile

yourself with it. Nor shall any woman stand before an animal to mate with it. It is perversion.

[24] "Do not defile yourselves with any of these things; for by all these the nations are defiled, which I am casting out before you. [25] For the land is defiled; therefore I visit the punishment of its iniquity upon it, and the land vomits out its inhabitants. [26] You shall therefore keep My statutes and My judgments, and shall not commit any of these abominations, either any of your own nation or any stranger who dwells among you [27] (for all these abominations the men of the land have done, who were before you, and thus the land is defiled), [28] lest the land vomit you out also when you defile it, as it vomited out the nations that were before you. [29] For whoever commits any of these abominations, *the persons who commit them shall be cut off from among their people*"

The above verses sentence all homosexuals to death! I must inform you that homosexuals are also part of God's creation. According to studies done by American researcher Alfred Kinsey some sixty years ago, a significant percentage of Earth's inhabitants are homosexuals. It simply cannot be that God didn't notice such a fact! There are many people who think homosexuality is a disease or perversion, but it is not so. A person is born homosexual, according to Dr. Weininger's research in the early 20th century, outlined in his book *Sex and Character* – I urge you to read it. God would have noticed this, and not created them at all if he thought they are not fit to live on this earth. He had made a similar decision in the past regarding circumcision when he suddenly decided that he had made a mistake when he created man and commanded Abraham to remove the foreskin of every son born. In the same way, using his marvelous powers, he could have healed the homosexuals and turned them straight, instead of sentencing a hefty portion of the world's population to death, simply because of a mistake he made. It seems religious people don't waste their time learning and acquiring new knowledge, but focus on important stuff – what all sorts of wise men have thought about God's creation. From the dawn of time there have been these wise men who sit and argue about their predecessors' opinions as they tried to explain what God supposedly said – when his very existence has never been proven by anyone. I myself have surprised many men of faith, of various religions, by asking them how many religions there are in the world today, to the best of their knowledge. When I told them there were thousands they were astounded, especially considering God has never appeared, not even by a hint, anywhere in the world ever since he created it.

19:1-8

¹And the Lord spoke to Moses, saying, ² "Speak to all the congregation of the children of Israel, and say to them: 'You shall be holy, for I the Lord your God am holy.
³ 'Every one of you shall revere his mother and his father, and keep My Sabbaths: I am the Lord your God.
⁴ 'Do not turn to idols, nor make for yourselves molded gods: I am the Lord your God.
⁵ 'And if you offer a sacrifice of a peace offering to the Lord, you shall offer it of your own free will. ⁶ It shall be eaten the same day you offer it, and on the next day. And if any remains until the third day, it shall be burned in the fire. ⁷ And if it is eaten at all on the third day, it is an abomination. It shall not be accepted. ⁸ Therefore everyone who eats it shall bear his iniquity, because he has profaned the hallowed offering of the Lord; and that person shall be cut off from his people.'

When you roast meat on the fire, you may eat the meat during the next two days only; whoever eats the meat on the third day shall be put to death! This law, along with the law requiring all slaughtering of animals to take place in the tabernacle of meeting, will essentially provide more food for the people in the tabernacle, especially Moses's people. But these days, when we have fridges and people keep meat in the freezer and eat it months later, this kind of law would wipe out all of the world's inhabitants. There are those in Israel who demand that instead of following state law we go back to living according to biblical law. I have already taken precautions, I have become a strict vegetarian.

19:9-22

[9] 'When you reap the harvest of your land, you shall not wholly reap the corners of your field, nor shall you gather the gleanings of your harvest. [10] And you shall not glean your vineyard, nor shall you gather every grape of your vineyard; you shall leave them for the poor and the stranger: I am the Lord your God.

[11] 'You shall not steal, nor deal falsely, nor lie to one another. [12] And you shall not swear by My name falsely, nor shall you profane the name of your God: I am the Lord.

[13] 'You shall not cheat your neighbor, nor rob him. The wages of him who is hired shall not remain with you all night until morning. [14] You shall not curse the deaf, nor put a stumbling block before the blind, but shall fear your God: I am the Lord.

[15] 'You shall do no injustice in judgment. You shall not be partial to the poor, nor honor the person of the mighty. In righteousness you shall judge your neighbor. [16] You shall not go about as a talebearer among your people; nor shall you take a stand against the life of your neighbor: I am the Lord.

[17] 'You shall not hate your brother in your heart. You shall surely rebuke your neighbor, and not bear sin because of him. [18] You shall not take vengeance, nor bear any grudge against the children of your people, but you shall love your neighbor as yourself: I am the Lord.

[19] 'You shall keep My statutes. You shall not let your livestock breed with another kind. You shall not sow your field with mixed seed. Nor shall a garment of mixed linen and wool come upon you.

[20] 'Whoever lies carnally with a woman who is betrothed to a man as a concubine, and who has not at all been redeemed, nor given her freedom, for this there shall be scourging; but they shall not be put to death, because she was not free. [21] And he shall bring his trespass offering to the Lord, to the door of

the tabernacle of meeting; a ram as a trespass offering. [22] The priest shall make atonement for him with the ram of the trespass offering before the Lord for his sin which he has committed. And the sin which he has committed shall be forgiven him.'"

The Israelites who left Egypt were shepherds, so that was their main occupation as they trekked through the desert. Due to the large quantities of meat consumed by Moses's army and their families, his entourage and their families, Aaron and his sons and their families, and all those who worked in the holy place and their families, Moses required a lot more meat than he received from sacrifices and presents. Besides, there were many people who preferred slaughtering their beasts without his supervision as they didn't want to give him the tithe or other cuts of meat that somehow disappeared during slaughter in the tabernacle. So Moses wrote Leviticus, which could also be called *Moses's Book of Meat*. Allegedly dictated to Moses by God, part of the book includes human laws that if broken are punishable with fines of meat, and strict instructions against slaughtering of animals outside the tabernacle of meeting; those who break these statutes are put to death. All this so that Moses could have complete control of the meat market.

21:16-23

[16] And the Lord spoke to Moses, saying, [17] "Speak to Aaron, saying: 'No man of your descendants in succeeding generations, who has any defect, may approach to offer the bread of his God. [18] For any man who has a defect shall not approach: a man blind or lame, who has a marred face or any limb too long, [19] a man who has a broken foot or broken hand, [20] or is a hunchback or a dwarf, or a man who has a defect in his eye, or eczema or scab, or is a eunuch. [21] No man of the descendants of Aaron the priest, who has a defect, shall come near to offer the offerings made by fire to the Lord. He has a defect; he shall not come near to offer the bread of his God. [22]

He may eat the bread of his God, both the most holy and the holy; [23] only he shall not go near the veil or approach the altar, because he has a defect, lest he profane My sanctuaries; for I the Lord sanctify them.'"

I can understand that the Lord God is not required to take care of each and every one of his creations, but Aaron's family whom he chose to work for him in the holy place forever more, surely they deserve special treatment. They received everything that God could give, so they deserve to be born whole in every way. Modern science today can, with a simple lab test, determine whether a pregnant woman is carrying a child with fetal abnormalities, and stop the pregnancy. According to these writings one understands that Moses did not like disabled people, so he forbade them from approaching the place he considered holy. If we consider that throughout the Israelites' journey in the desert there is no mention of handicapped people, we can assume that Moses had probably taken care of them already.

22:28

[28] "Whether it is a cow or ewe, do not kill both her and her young on the same day."

Once more we see a humane law similar to 'you shall not boil a young goat in its mother's milk', which was somehow interpreted in a way that defies logical, sensible thinking.

23:1-3

[1] And the Lord spoke to Moses, saying, [2] "Speak to the children of Israel, and say to them: 'The feasts of the Lord, which you shall proclaim to be holy convocations, these are My feasts.
[3] 'Six days shall work be done, but the seventh day is a Sabbath of solemn rest, a holy convocation. You shall do no work on it; it is the Sabbath of the Lord in all your dwellings.'"

This verse takes us back to the ten commandments, so I think it only fitting to go back and reread the ten commandments. I have noticed that the commandments include a few general statutes such as: honor your father and your mother; you shall not covet your neighbor's wife, nor his male servant, nor his female servant, nor his ox, nor his donkey, nor anything that is your neighbor's; and remember the Sabbath day, to keep it holy. Six days you shall labor and do all your work, but the seventh day is the Sabbath of the Lord your God; from these generalizations I understand that you cannot follow only part of any commandment; you cannot honor your father without also honoring your mother, or not covet your neighbor's wife, but covet his ox and donkey. Most importantly, you cannot separate keeping the Sabbath holy from its most vital counterpart for life on earth, that is – six days you shall labor! So keeping the Sabbath is meaningless without the previous six days of work. This is precisely how God behaved as he set an example, which is why he also wrote it down. So anyone who says they keep the Sabbath but does not work the six days prior -- why this person does not believe in God at all!

In addition, I notice that in the last few chapters Moses repeats the importance of keeping the Sabbath over and over again, sentencing any who do not keep it holy to be put to death. Not only did he never link the Sabbath with the six days of labor, but I find it difficult to understand why he took such an extreme view of one half of this commandment. After all, the great majority of the world's inhabitants have chosen to overlook this part entirely while accepting the other commandments, and the more important half of this one, that Moses chose to disregard for some reason – 'six days shall you labor'. I am perplexed, how can anyone make a living without work. And let us not forget that God himself set an example, which is why he wrote the commandments in a certain order. First, believe in God wholeheartedly, second go work -- don't make excuses; honor your parents who brought you up to follow the straight and narrow path rather than have you murder, commit adultery, steal, lie, or covet any and all things. Simply go work.

23:6-8

[6] "And on the fifteenth day of the same month is the Feast of Unleavened Bread to the Lord; seven days you must eat unleavened bread. [7] On the first day you shall have a holy convocation; you shall do no customary work on it. [8] But you shall offer an offering made by fire to the Lord for seven days."

In special cases we are allowed to light a fire and roast meat even on Saturday. I might have ignored this part if it weren't for Moses's fanatic devotion to the death penalty for anyone who doesn't keep the Sabbath. So it begs the question – why? It seems many of the Israelites preferred to slaughter their beasts without donating a cut to the tabernacle of meeting. So they left the camp on Saturday – the day designated for rest – to slaughter their animals, which had a strong negative effect on the meat market controlled by Moses. This could be one of a few possible explanations, based on the turn of events at the time. Moreover, the number of people who worked in the holy place kept growing, so there were more people to feed. The liberated slaves, crossing the desert with their herds, were tired after a long day's work and could not concentrate on serving gourmet food in the tabernacle of meeting.

17:1-4

[1]And the Lord spoke to Moses, saying, [2] "Speak to Aaron, to his sons, and to all the children of Israel, and say to them, 'This is the thing which the Lord has commanded, saying: [3] Whatever man of the house of Israel who kills an ox or lamb or goat in the camp, or who kills it outside the camp, [4] and does not bring it to the door of the tabernacle of meeting to offer an offering to the Lord before the tabernacle of the Lord, the guilt

of bloodshed shall be imputed to that man. He has shed blood; and that man shall be cut off from among his people.'"

17:8-9

...⁸"Whatever man of the house of Israel, or of the strangers who dwell among you, who offers a burnt offering or sacrifice, ⁹ and does not bring it to the door of the tabernacle of meeting, to offer it to the Lord, that man shall be cut off from among his people."

Knowing there was meat that was not brought to the tabernacle of meeting made Moses furious. He therefore decided that anyone who disobeyed 'God's command' will be sentenced to death. When it came to meat Moses had no qualms about cruel and unusual punishment, despite 'Thou shalt not kill'.

23:9-14

9 And the Lord spoke to Moses, saying, **¹⁰** "Speak to the children of Israel, and say to them: 'When you come into the land which I give to you, and reap its harvest, then you shall bring a sheaf of the first fruits of your harvest to the priest. **¹¹** He shall wave the sheaf before the Lord, to be accepted on your behalf; on the day after the Sabbath the priest shall wave it. **¹²** And you shall offer on that day, when you wave the sheaf, a male lamb of the first year, without blemish, as a burnt offering to the Lord. **¹³** Its grain offering shall be two-tenths of an ephah of fine flour mixed with oil, an offering made by fire to the Lord, for a sweet aroma; and its drink offering shall be of wine, one-fourth of a hin. **¹⁴** You shall eat neither bread nor parched grain nor fresh grain until the same day that you have brought an offering to your God; it shall be a statute forever throughout your generations in all your dwellings.

23:15-20

[15] 'And you shall count for yourselves from the day after the Sabbath, from the day that you brought the sheaf of the wave offering: seven Sabbaths shall be completed. [16] Count fifty days to the day after the seventh Sabbath; then you shall offer a new grain offering to the Lord. [17] You shall bring from your dwellings two wave loaves of two-tenths of an ephah. They shall be of fine flour; they shall be baked with leaven. They are the first fruits to the Lord. [18] And you shall offer with the bread seven lambs of the first year, without blemish, one young bull, and two rams. They shall be as a burnt offering to the Lord, with their grain offering and their drink offerings, an offering made by fire for a sweet aroma to the Lord. [19] Then you shall sacrifice one kid of the goats as a sin offering, and two male lambs of the first year as a sacrifice of a peace offering. [20] The priest shall wave them with the bread of the firstfruits as a wave offering before the Lord, with the two lambs. They shall be holy to the Lord for the priest.'"

One can't help wondering whether the Israelites brought all these foods to the tabernacle of meeting of their own free will, or whether this is another instance of coercion. I find it hard to believe that shepherds are so stupid that they would be willing to support a parasitic circle of people that keeps growing and growing (based on the increasing amount of food ordered by God).

23:23-25

[23] Then the Lord spoke to Moses, saying, [24] "Speak to the children of Israel, saying: 'In the seventh month, on the first day of the month, you shall have a sabbath-rest, a memorial of blowing of trumpets, a holy convocation. [25] You shall do no customary work on it; and you shall offer an offering made by fire to the Lord.'"

'And you shall offer an offering made by fire to the Lord', is an abstruse sentence. However, this is a task that is not affected by the day of the week, and must be performed each and every day, even on Saturday. I have tried to understand this command, but every book I have searched directed me to another book, which directed me to yet another book and so on, so I am still baffled by its meaning.

23:33-38

[33] Then the Lord spoke to Moses, saying, [34] "Speak to the children of Israel, saying: 'The fifteenth day of this seventh month shall be the Feast of Tabernacles for seven days to the Lord. [35] On the first day there shall be a holy convocation. You shall do no customary work on it. [36] For seven days you shall offer an offering made by fire to the Lord. On the eighth day you shall have a holy convocation, and you shall offer an offering made by fire to the Lord. It is a sacred assembly, and you shall do no customary work on it.
[37] 'These are the feasts of the Lord which you shall proclaim to be holy convocations, to offer an offering made by fire to the Lord, a burnt offering and a grain offering, a sacrifice and drink offerings, everything on its day—[38] besides the Sabbaths of the Lord, besides your gifts, besides all your vows, and besides all your freewill offerings which you give to the Lord.'"

10:12-13

[12] And Moses spoke to Aaron, and to Eleazar and Ithamar, his sons who were left: "Take the grain offering that remains of the offerings made by fire to the Lord, and eat it without leaven beside the altar; for it is most holy. [13] You shall eat it in a holy place, because it is your due and your sons' due, of the sacrifices made by fire to the Lord; for so I have been commanded."

23:26-27

26 And the Lord spoke to Moses, saying: **27** "Also the tenth day of this seventh month shall be the Day of Atonement. It shall be a holy convocation for you; you shall afflict your souls, and offer an offering made by fire to the Lord."

Moses gives Aaron's remaining sons (after their brothers Nadab and Abihu died because they used profane fire) permission to eat from God's offerings. It turns out that this is a sacrifice of meat and other delicacies which are offered to God alone every day without fail, including Saturdays and even Yom Kippur. It is clear that Moses gives his permission without receiving God's consent – no longer does it say "and the Lord spoke to Moses". I do not recall such an incident in the past where Moses took such heavy responsibility. Perhaps it is simply absentmindedness, and Moses forgot to write, 'And the Lord spoke to Moses'.

24:1-9

Then the Lord spoke to Moses, saying: **2** "Command the children of Israel that they bring to you pure oil of pressed olives for the light, to make the lamps burn continually. **3** Outside the veil of the Testimony, in the tabernacle of meeting, Aaron shall be in charge of it from evening until morning before the Lord continually; it shall be a statute forever in your generations. **4** He shall be in charge of the lamps on the pure gold lampstand before the Lord continually.
5 "And you shall take fine flour and bake twelve cakes with it. Two-tenths of an ephah shall be in each cake. **6** You shall set them in two rows, six in a row, on the pure gold table before the Lord. **7** And you shall put pure frankincense on each row, that it may be on the bread for a memorial, an offering made by fire to the Lord. **8** Every Sabbath he shall set it in order before the Lord continually, being taken from the children of Israel by an everlasting covenant. **9** And it shall be for Aaron and his sons, and they shall eat it in a holy place; for it is most

holy to him from the offerings of the Lord made by fire, by a perpetual statute."

The constant mention of foods that must be served to God portrays him as a glutton. It is absolutely impossible that there is any truth in these words. It can all be attributed to a cruel tyrant who surrounded himself with followers and family, took over and exploited a people of slaves. Moses led them through the desert, assuring them that he was leading them to the promised land, an assurance which he probably meant to keep. But as time wore on it seems he changed his mind, and his actions accordingly. We might also note that Moses had no reason to hurry and bring the people to the Promised Land; Moses appointed himself supreme god, and of course as God's chosen messenger his family, entourage and followers enjoyed all the privileges and comforts available during the trek through the desert. Moses's control over the people was absolute.

Numbers

1:1-3

[1] Now the Lord spoke to Moses in the Wilderness of Sinai, in the tabernacle of meeting, on the first day of the second month, in the second year after they had come out of the land of Egypt, saying: [2] "Take a census of all the congregation of the children of Israel, by their families, by their fathers' houses, according to the number of names, every male individually, [3] from twenty years old and above—all who are able to go to war in Israel. You and Aaron shall number them by their armies."

The book of Numbers begins with Moses deciding to conduct a census of all the tribes, by organizing all ex-army men aged twenty and up in each tribe. When the census reaches the Levy tribe, it becomes conclusively apparent that Moses indeed had a private army of his own. The number of males aged one month and up was 22,000. Add to that all the women of all ages, and babies under one month, and it becomes clear that there was a large number of people needing food, lots of food, not to mention other needs. This clarifies why 'God' kept asking Moses to provide 'Him' with so much food – which continued to increase in quantity and quality as the tribe grew. The nature of other steps taken by Moses also becomes clear: his taking over the meat market; the demand to carry out the sacrifice only by the tabernacle of meeting rather than outside the camp; the obligation of giving a tithe to the staff of the tabernacle of meeting. The strict laws concerning observing the Sabbath, with the ensuing death penalty for breaking them, also came to increase the amount of meat earmarked for the tabernacle of meeting, as were the laws of sacrificing to God a tithe of all produce. All have the same aim: providing food for the group doing the holy work and their families. We can therefore conclude that the people's belief in the Lord was of utmost importance to Moses; without it, he would have lost control over the people.

1:48-54

[48] For the Lord had spoken to Moses, saying: [49] "Only the tribe of Levi you shall not number, nor take a census of them among the children of Israel; [50] but you shall appoint the Levites over the tabernacle of the Testimony, over all its furnishings, and over all things that belong to it; they shall carry the tabernacle and all its furnishings; they shall attend to it and camp around the tabernacle. [51] And when the tabernacle is to go forward, the Levites shall take it down; and when the tabernacle is to be set up, the Levites shall set it up. The outsider who comes near shall be put to death. [52] The children of Israel shall pitch their tents, everyone by his own camp, everyone by his own standard, according to their armies; [53] but the Levites shall camp around the tabernacle of the Testimony, that there may be no wrath on the congregation of the children of Israel; and the Levites shall keep charge of the tabernacle of the Testimony."

[54] Thus the children of Israel did; according to all that the Lord commanded Moses, so they did.

This is where God distinctly appoints the Tribe of Levy as guardians of the tabernacle. The tribe is divided into three groups, each with its own function such as striking camp, setting it up, carrying the tent's components during transit, and so on – all to be done by the Levites only.

3:5-10

[5] And the Lord spoke to Moses, saying: [6] "Bring the tribe of Levi near, and present them before Aaron the priest, that they may serve him. [7] And they shall attend to his needs and the needs of the whole congregation before the tabernacle of meeting, to do the work of the tabernacle. [8] Also they shall attend to all the furnishings of the tabernacle of meeting, and

to the needs of the children of Israel, to do the work of the tabernacle. [9] And you shall give the Levites to Aaron and his sons; they are given entirely to him from among the children of Israel. [10] So you shall appoint Aaron and his sons, and they shall attend to their priesthood; but the outsider who comes near shall be put to death."

Here again is an irrational death sentence for an incomprehensible offense. What could be so secret in the tabernacle, to merit Moses hiding it? I've given deep thought to this question, and discovered the reason for secrecy: In the tent was the altar on which the sacrifices to the Lord were made. The altar contained capacious drawers on either side, into which the 'sacrifices' given 'to the Lord' were channeled, according to type: a drawer for the clean, salted meat; another for fine flour in oil; a third for wine; and so forth. After all, you readers in the 21st century don't continue believing that God really ate so much food; a tenth of all the produce and the cattle and sheep would be huge quantities fit for a large army, as well as their kith and kin. This is what Moses wanted to hide from nosy busybodies, and this is why he ordered the death penalty, as he did on previous occasions such as approaching Mt Sinai.

Exodus 19:12

[12] You shall set bounds for the people all around, saying, "Take heed to yourselves that you do not go up to the mountain or touch its base. Whoever touches the mountain shall surely be put to death."

To this we may add the contraption for producing smoke during the day and a large flame at night, a device which Moses obviously didn't want people to see.

3:44-51

⁴⁴ Then the Lord spoke to Moses, saying: ⁴⁵ "Take the Levites instead of all the firstborn among the children of Israel, and the livestock of the Levites instead of their livestock. The Levites shall be Mine: I am the Lord. ⁴⁶ And for the redemption of the two hundred and seventy-three of the firstborn of the children of Israel, who are more than the number of the Levites, ⁴⁷ you shall take five shekels for each one individually; you shall take them in the currency of the shekel of the sanctuary, the shekel of twenty gerahs. ⁴⁸ And you shall give the money, with which the excess number of them is redeemed, to Aaron and his sons."

⁴⁹ So Moses took the redemption money from those who were over and above those who were redeemed by the Levites. ⁵⁰ From the firstborn of the children of Israel he took the money, one thousand three hundred and sixty-five shekels, according to the shekel of the sanctuary. ⁵¹ And Moses gave their redemption money to Aaron and his sons, according to the word of the Lord, as the Lord commanded Moses.

It has been a year and one month since the Israelites left Egypt, and Moses continues to scheme and find ways to divest the people of their hard-earned money and the fruit of their labor, just as is done to the public to this very day. At this point, not surprisingly, the Lord tells Moses to tax each eldest son with five shekels, for the benefit of the Levites. However, he then transfers that money to Aaron & Sons, who just happen to be his brother and nephews. I must reiterate that all this preoccupation with meat and cash on the part of God totally negates his existence as a Supreme God. But let's leave that issue to the consideration of the intelligent reader and his innate level of antagonism. The interesting aspect of this issue is that Moses sees the need to record all these details, even if they're in contradiction with this earlier actions.

5:11-31

[11] And the Lord spoke to Moses, saying, [12] "Speak to the children of Israel, and say to them: 'If any man's wife goes astray and behaves unfaithfully toward him, [13] and a man lies with her carnally, and it is hidden from the eyes of her husband, and it is concealed that she has defiled herself, and there was no witness against her, nor was she caught— [14] if the spirit of jealousy comes upon him and he becomes jealous of his wife, who has defiled herself; or if the spirit of jealousy comes upon him and he becomes jealous of his wife, although she has not defiled herself— [15] then the man shall bring his wife to the priest. He shall bring the offering required for her, one-tenth of an ephah of barley meal; he shall pour no oil on it and put no frankincense on it, because it is a grain offering of jealousy, an offering for remembering, for bringing iniquity to remembrance.

[16] 'And the priest shall bring her near, and set her before the Lord. [17] The priest shall take holy water in an earthen vessel, and take some of the dust that is on the floor of the tabernacle and put it into the water. [18] Then the priest shall stand the woman before the Lord, uncover the woman's head, and put the offering for remembering in her hands, which is the grain offering of jealousy. And the priest shall have in his hand the bitter water that brings a curse. [19] And the priest shall put her under oath, and say to the woman, "If no man has lain with you, and if you have not gone astray to uncleanness while under your husband's authority, be free from this bitter water that brings a curse. [20] But if you have gone astray while under your husband's authority, and if you have defiled yourself and some man other than your husband has lain with you"— [21] then the priest shall put the woman under the oath of the curse, and he shall say to the woman—"the Lord make you a curse and an oath among your people, when the Lord makes your thigh rot and your belly swell; [22] and may this water that causes the curse go into your stomach, and make your belly swell and your thigh rot."

'Then the woman shall say, "Amen, so be it."

23 'Then the priest shall write these curses in a book, and he shall scrape them off into the bitter water. 24 And he shall make the woman drink the bitter water that brings a curse, and the water that brings the curse shall enter her to become bitter. 25 Then the priest shall take the grain offering of jealousy from the woman's hand, shall wave the offering before the Lord, and bring it to the altar; 26 and the priest shall take a handful of the offering, as its memorial portion, burn it on the altar, and afterward make the woman drink the water. 27 When he has made her drink the water, then it shall be, if she has defiled herself and behaved unfaithfully toward her husband, that the water that brings a curse will enter her and become bitter, and her belly will swell, her thigh will rot, and the woman will become a curse among her people. 28 But if the woman has not defiled herself, and is clean, then she shall be free and may conceive children.

29 'This is the law of jealousy, when a wife, while under her husband's authority, goes astray and defiles herself, 30 or when the spirit of jealousy comes upon a man, and he becomes jealous of his wife; then he shall stand the woman before the Lord, and the priest shall execute all this law upon her. 31 Then the man shall be free from iniquity, but that woman shall bear her guilt.'"

I fail to see the connection between a woman's act of unfaithfulness to her husband, the husband's fit of jealousy, and holy water, or bitter water, or any other kind of water.

This reminds me of a case in my own life. My daughter, when separating from her husband, asked me to sign a certain financial guarantee for her. I went to the local Rabbinate, where the signing was to take place. I entered the small cubicle where the old man, presumably a rabbi, sat. His face was covered in a white beard, yellowing around the mouth. His two assistants, in their twenties, sat on either side, and all were engulfed in heavy cigarette smoke emanating from the rabbi, who was puffing away at tremendous speed that even I, as an ex-heavy smoker, wasn't familiar with. The young men sat slightly diagonally and away from the smoking rabbi, their discomfort evident on their faces. I approached the counter, which was about the same height as a bank teller's, and the rabbi asked for my ID details and proffered me the document and a pen. I reached for the pen with my left hand, but the rabbi wouldn't give it to me, saying I had to hold it in my right hand, even though I'm left-handed. In this case – explained the rabbi – I must take the pen in my right hand, transfer it to the left for signing, then transfer it back to the right hand and thus return it to the rabbi.

I have had occasion to come across many strange phenomena, but this was one of the strangest. Until then, having been brought up in a religious family, I held religious people in high regard.

As for the use of holy water, it's very common in Israel to this very day; it's even one of our exports – water from the Holy Land. Fact is, there is a demand, there are plenty of customers.

6:1-20

[1] Then the lord spoke to Moses, saying, [2] "Speak to the children of Israel, and say to them: 'When either a man or woman consecrates an offering to take the vow of a Nazirite, to separate himself to the Lord, [3] he shall separate himself from wine and similar drink; he shall drink neither vinegar made from wine nor vinegar made from similar drink; neither shall he drink any grape juice, nor eat fresh grapes or raisins. [4] All the days of his separation he shall eat nothing that is produced by the grapevine, from seed to skin.

[5] 'All the days of the vow of his separation no razor shall come upon his head; until the days are fulfilled for which he separated himself to the Lord, he shall be holy. Then he shall let the locks of the hair of his head grow. [6] All the days that he separates himself to the Lord he shall not go near a dead body. [7] He shall not make himself unclean even for his father or his mother, for his brother or his sister, when they die, because his separation to God is on his head. [8] All the days of his separation he shall be holy to the Lord.

⁹ 'And if anyone dies very suddenly beside him, and he defiles his consecrated head, then he shall shave his head on the day of his cleansing; on the seventh day he shall shave it. ¹⁰ Then on the eighth day he shall bring two turtledoves or two young pigeons to the priest, to the door of the tabernacle of meeting; ¹¹ and the priest shall offer one as a sin offering and the other as a burnt offering, and make atonement for him, because he sinned in regard to the corpse; and he shall sanctify his head that same day. ¹² He shall consecrate to the Lord the days of his separation, and bring a male lamb in its first year as a trespass offering; but the former days shall be lost, because his separation was defiled.

¹³ 'Now this is the law of the Nazirite: When the days of his separation are fulfilled, he shall be brought to the door of the tabernacle of meeting. ¹⁴ And he shall present his offering to the Lord: one male lamb in its first year without blemish as a burnt offering, one ewe lamb in its first year without blemish as a sin offering, one ram without blemish as a peace offering, ¹⁵ a basket of unleavened bread, cakes of fine flour mixed with oil, unleavened wafers anointed with oil, and their grain offering with their drink offerings.

¹⁶ 'Then the priest shall bring them before the Lord and offer his sin offering and his burnt offering; ¹⁷ and he shall offer the ram as a sacrifice of a peace offering to the Lord, with the basket of unleavened bread; the priest shall also offer its grain offering and its drink offering. ¹⁸ Then the Nazirite shall shave his consecrated head at the door of the tabernacle of meeting, and shall take the hair from his consecrated head and put it on the fire which is under the sacrifice of the peace offering.

¹⁹ 'And the priest shall take the boiled shoulder of the ram, one unleavened cake from the basket, and one unleavened wafer, and put them upon the hands of the Nazirite after he has shaved his consecrated hair, ²⁰ and the priest shall wave them as a wave offering before the Lord; they are holy for the priest, together with the breast of the wave offering and the thigh of the heave offering. After that the Nazirite may drink wine.'"

Usually, when I'm facing a financial outlay for a certain purchase or job, I first check whether I can do it myself – for reasons of economy. Therefore, when I wished to take a vow (for personal reasons which shall remain unspecified) and realized I couldn't do it on my own, I approached the authorized people and presented them with my wish to take a vow. Being one of those who ask 'How much is this gonna cost me?', I was given the list shown below:

- Two turtle-doves or two young pigeons
- A male lamb in its first year
- Another lamb in its first year
- One ewe lamb in its first year without blemish
- One ram without blemish as a peace offering
- Basket of unleavened bread
- Cakes of fine flour mixed with oil
- Unleavened wafers anointed with oil

While contemplating the list, I completely forgot what was the vow I wanted to take. That's one way of economizing.

7:11

[11] For the Lord said to Moses, "They shall offer their offering, one leader each day, for the dedication of the altar."

To celebrate the dedication of the new altar in the tabernacle, the Lord arranges the order in which the leaders of the various tribes should come, to offer their sacrifices to him:

7:12-17

[12] And the one who offered his offering on the first day was Nahshon the son of Amminadab, from the tribe of Judah. [13] His offering was one silver platter, the weight of which was one hundred and thirty shekels, and one silver bowl of seventy shekels, according to the shekel of the sanctuary, both of them full of fine flour mixed with oil as a grain offering; [14] one gold

pan of ten shekels, full of incense; [15] one young bull, one ram, and one male lamb in its first year, as a burnt offering; [16] one kid of the goats as a sin offering; [17] and for the sacrifice of peace offerings: two oxen, five rams, five male goats, and five male lambs in their first year. This was the offering of Nahshon the son of Amminadab.

7:18-23

[18] On the second day Nethanel the son of Zuar, leader of Issachar, presented an offering. [19] For his offering he offered one silver platter, the weight of which was one hundred and thirty shekels, and one silver bowl of seventy shekels, according to the shekel of the sanctuary, both of them full of fine flour mixed with oil as a grain offering; [20] one gold pan of ten shekels, full of incense; [21] one young bull, one ram, and one male lamb in its first year, as a burnt offering; [22] one kid of the goats as a sin offering; [23] and as the sacrifice of peace offerings: two oxen, five rams, five male goats, and five male lambs in their first year. This was the offering of Nethanel the son of Zuar.

7:24-29

[24] On the third day Eliab the son of Helon, leader of the children of Zebulun, presented an offering.[25] His offering was one silver platter, the weight of which was one hundred and thirty shekels, and one silver bowl of seventy shekels, according to the shekel of the sanctuary, both of them full of fine flour mixed with oil as a grain offering;[26] one gold pan of ten shekels, full of incense;[27] one young bull, one ram, and one male lamb in its first year, as a burnt offering; [28] one kid of the goats as a sin offering; [29] and for the sacrifice of peace offerings: two oxen, five rams, five male goats, and five male lambs in their first year. This was the offering of Eliab the son of Helon.

7:30-35

³⁰ On the fourth day Elizur the son of Shedeur, leader of the children of Reuben, presented an offering. ³¹ His offering was one silver platter, the weight of which was one hundred and thirty shekels, and one silver bowl of seventy shekels, according to the shekel of the sanctuary, both of them full of fine flour mixed with oil as a grain offering; ³² one gold pan of ten shekels, full of incense; ³³ one young bull, one ram, and one male lamb in its first year, as a burnt offering; ³⁴ one kid of the goats as a sin offering; ³⁵ and as the sacrifice of peace offerings: two oxen, five rams, five male goats, and five male lambs in their first year. This was the offering of Elizur the son of Shedeur.

7:36-41

³⁶ On the fifth day Shelumiel the son of Zurishaddai, leader of the children of Simeon, presented an offering. ³⁷ His offering was one silver platter, the weight of which was one hundred and thirty shekels, and one silver bowl of seventy shekels, according to the shekel of the sanctuary, both of them full of fine flour mixed with oil as a grain offering; ³⁸ one gold pan of ten shekels, full of incense; ³⁹ one young bull, one ram, and one male lamb in its first year, as a burnt offering; ⁴⁰ one kid of the goats as a sin offering; ⁴¹ and as the sacrifice of peace offerings: two oxen, five rams, five male goats, and five male lambs in their first year. This was the offering of Shelumiel the son of Zurishaddai.

7:42-47

⁴² On the sixth day Eliasaph the son of Deuel,[b] leader of the children of Gad, presented an offering. ⁴³ His offering was one silver platter, the weight of which was one hundred and thirty shekels, and one silver bowl of seventy shekels, according to the shekel of the sanctuary, both of them full of fine flour mixed with oil as a grain offering; ⁴⁴ one gold pan of

ten shekels, full of incense; [45] one young bull, one ram, and one male lamb in its first year, as a burnt offering;[46] one kid of the goats as a sin offering; [47] and as the sacrifice of peace offerings: two oxen, five rams, five male goats, and five male lambs in their first year. This was the offering of Eliasaph the son of Deuel.

7:54-59

[54] On the eighth day Gamaliel the son of Pedahzur, leader of the children of Manasseh, presented an offering. [55] His offering was one silver platter, the weight of which was one hundred and thirty shekels, and one silver bowl of seventy shekels, according to the shekel of the sanctuary, both of them full of fine flour mixed with oil as a grain offering; [56] one gold pan of ten shekels, full of incense; [57] one young bull, one ram, and one male lamb in its first year, as a burnt offering; [58] one kid of the goats as a sin offering; [59] and as the sacrifice of peace offerings: two oxen, five rams, five male goats, and five male lambs in their first year. This was the offering of Gamaliel the son of Pedahzur.

7:60-65

[60] On the ninth day Abidan the son of Gideoni, leader of the children of Benjamin, presented an offering. [61] His offering was one silver platter, the weight of which was one hundred and thirty shekels, and one silver bowl of seventy shekels, according to the shekel of the sanctuary, both of them full of fine flour mixed with oil as a grain offering; [62] one gold pan of ten shekels, full of incense; [63] one young bull, one ram, and one male lamb in its first year, as a burnt offering;[64] one kid of the goats as a sin offering; [65] and as the sacrifice of peace offerings: two oxen, five rams, five male goats, and five male lambs in their first year. This was the offering of Abidan the son of Gideoni.

7:66-71

⁶⁶ On the tenth day Ahiezer the son of Ammishaddai, leader of the children of Dan, presented an offering. ⁶⁷ His offering was one silver platter, the weight of which was one hundred and thirty shekels, and one silver bowl of seventy shekels, according to the shekel of the sanctuary, both of them full of fine flour mixed with oil as a grain offering; ⁶⁸ one gold pan of ten shekels, full of incense; ⁶⁹ one young bull, one ram, and one male lamb in its first year, as a burnt offering; ⁷⁰ one kid of the goats as a sin offering; ⁷¹ and as the sacrifice of peace offerings: two oxen, five rams, five male goats, and five male lambs in their first year. This was the offering of Ahiezer the son of Ammishaddai.

7:72-77

⁷² On the eleventh day Pagiel the son of Ocran, leader of the children of Asher, presented an offering. ⁷³ His offering was one silver platter, the weight of which was one hundred and thirty shekels, and one silver bowl of seventy shekels, according to the shekel of the sanctuary, both of them full of fine flour mixed with oil as a grain offering; ⁷⁴ one gold pan of ten shekels, full of incense; ⁷⁵ one young bull, one ram, and one male lamb in its first year, as a burnt offering;⁷⁶ one kid of the goats as a sin offering; ⁷⁷ and as the sacrifice of peace offerings: two oxen, five rams, five male goats, and five male lambs in their first year. This was the offering of Pagiel the son of Ocran.

All this clearly indicates how the Lord arranges the queue in an orderly fashion, according to the names of the leaders of the tribes of Israel; and naturally, each leader must contribute something to the dedication ceremony, and all this is written down by Moses, since only he can receive instructions from the Lord and pass them on.

7:78-83

⁷⁸ On the twelfth day Ahira the son of Enan, leader of the children of Naphtali, presented an offering. ⁷⁹ His offering was one silver platter, the weight of which was one hundred and thirty shekels, and one silver bowl of seventy shekels, according to the shekel of the sanctuary, both of them full of fine flour mixed with oil as a grain offering; ⁸⁰ one gold pan of ten shekels, full of incense; ⁸¹ one young bull, one ram, and one male lamb in its first year, as a burnt offering; ⁸² one kid of the goats as a sin offering; ⁸³ and as the sacrifice of peace offerings: two oxen, five rams, five male goats, and five male lambs in their first year. This was the offering of Ahira the son of Enan.

7:84-88

⁸⁴ This was the dedication offering for the altar from the leaders of Israel, when it was anointed: twelve silver platters, twelve silver bowls, and twelve gold pans. ⁸⁵ Each silver platter weighed one hundred and thirty shekels and each bowl seventy shekels. All the silver of the vessels weighed two thousand four hundred shekels, according to the shekel of the sanctuary. ⁸⁶ The twelve gold pans full of incense weighed ten shekels apiece, according to the shekel of the sanctuary; all the gold of the pans weighed one hundred and twenty shekels. ⁸⁷ All the oxen for the burnt offering were twelve young bulls, the rams twelve, the male lambs in their first year twelve, with their grain offering, and the kids of the goats as a sin offering twelve. ⁸⁸ And all the oxen for the sacrifice of peace offerings were twenty-four bulls, the rams sixty, the male goats sixty, and the lambs in their first year sixty. This was the dedication offering for the altar after it was anointed.

This is an impressive collection of donations which can encourage people who might want to join or take part in the leadership and in dividing the accumulated wealth. This is quite legitimate in a democratic society, but not with Moses.

9:6-8

⁶ Now there were certain men who were defiled by a human corpse, so that they could not keep the Passover on that day; and they came before Moses and Aaron that day. ⁷ And those men said to him, "We became defiled by a human corpse. Why are we kept from presenting the offering of the Lord at its appointed time among the children of Israel?"

⁸ And Moses said to them, "Stand still, that I may hear what the Lord will command concerning you."

Moses is not one to turn down an offer of meat... He may have been shocked by the mere request, but takes care to include God and his input in his decision.

9:15-19

¹⁵ Now on the day that the tabernacle was raised up, the cloud covered the tabernacle, the tent of the Testimony; from evening until morning it was above the tabernacle like the appearance of fire. ¹⁶ So it was always: the cloud covered it by day, and the appearance of fire by night. ¹⁷ Whenever the cloud was taken up from above the tabernacle, after that the children of Israel would journey; and in the place where the cloud settled, there the children of Israel would pitch their tents. ¹⁸ At the command of the Lord the children of Israel would journey, and at the command of the Lord they would camp; as long as the cloud stayed above the tabernacle they remained encamped. ¹⁹ Even when the cloud continued long, many days above the tabernacle, the children of Israel kept the charge of the Lord and did not journey.

Moses uses his pyrotechnical skills to create the effect of the pillar of smoke by day and pillar of fire by night; both in order to reinforce the faith in his followers and perhaps to persuade and enlist new believers.

10:29-32

²⁹ Now Moses said to Hobab the son of Reuel[a] the Midianite, Moses's father-in-law, "We are setting out for the place of which the Lord said, 'I will give it to you.' Come with us, and we will treat you well; for the Lord has promised good things to Israel."
³⁰ And he said to him, "I will not go, but I will depart to my own land and to my relatives."
³¹ So Moses said, "Please do not leave, inasmuch as you know how we are to camp in the wilderness, and you can be our eyes. ³² And it shall be, if you go with us—indeed it shall be—that whatever good the Lord will do to us, the same we will do to you."

Moses approaches Hobab, son of Reuel, i.e. the son of his in-law Jethro, asking him to guide him on his way to the Promised Land. Moses even tries to bribe Hobab by promising him he'll share with him whatever God gives him upon reaching their destination. But the fellow refuses, and wants simply to return to his native land. Could it be that Hobab is already familiar with Moses and all his tricks? Note that Moses himself didn't really believe in the pillars of smoke and fire that he created with his pyrotechnical skills. It's also interesting that Moses records these two events in one chapter; which shows Moses' low opinion of people's intelligence; though he may have a point in that line of thinking.

11:1-2

¹ Now when the people complained, it displeased the Lord; for the Lord heard it, and His anger was aroused. So the fire of the Lord burned among them, and consumed some in the outskirts of the camp. ² Then the people cried out to Moses, and when Moses prayed to the Lord, the fire was quenched.

Moses didn't like the people's complaints against him or against the Lord, and elimination is the only method he uses;

in this case, the elimination of the weak, the old and the disabled, who usually struggle at the edges of the camp, and the need to care for them dispirits Moses. The constant dealing with slaughtering cattle doesn't calm him down, either. Anyway, it seems that from time to time Moses needs to satisfy his need for letting blood, whether human blood or animal blood. This may be the place to add that nowhere in the Torah does it say how the weak, sick or injured among the people were treated along the way.

11:4-15

[1] So the children of Israel also wept again and said: "Who will give us meat to eat? [5] We remember the fish which we ate freely in Egypt, the cucumbers, the melons, the leeks, the onions, and the garlic;[6] but now our whole being is dried up; there is nothing at all except this manna before our eyes!"

[7] Now the manna was like coriander seed, and its color like the color of bdellium. [8] The people went about and gathered it, ground it on millstones or beat it in the mortar, cooked it in pans, and made cakes of it; and its taste was like the taste of pastry prepared with oil. [9] And when the dew fell on the camp in the night, the manna fell on it.

[10] Then Moses heard the people weeping throughout their families, everyone at the door of his tent; and the anger of the Lord was greatly aroused; Moses also was displeased. [11] So Moses said to the Lord, "Why have You afflicted Your servant? And why have I not found favor in Your sight, that You have laid the burden of all these people on me? [12] Did I conceive all these people? Did I beget them, that You should say to me, 'Carry them in your bosom, as a guardian carries a nursing child,' to the land which You swore to their fathers? [13] Where am I to get meat to give to all these people? For they weep all over me, saying, 'Give us meat, that we may eat.' [14] I am not able to bear all these people alone, because the burden is too heavy for me. [15] If You treat me like this, please kill me here and now—if I have found favor in Your sight—and do not let me see my wretchedness!"

Moses pretends to be very sensitive to the people's sufferings due to having nothing to eat except the manna, of which they'd grown tired. Moses complains to the Lord that he supposedly hasn't enough meat to feed the people.

Apparently, Moses escaped from Egypt to the desert, after getting involved in an event about which there are few details. In the desert, he met Jethro and married his daughter Zipporah. Jethro, a shepherd, takes Moses into the family business, and together they tend their flocks, traversing the desert in search of good pastures. This is how Moses got to know the desert well, through all seasons. From the text it seems that Moses is the one writing his life story, and he mentions at the beginning of each event that it is God who guides him and tells him what to do. Except for a few cases of forgetfulness... But sometimes it is Moses who advises God or even argues with him. However, it is very important to Moses to turn the entire people into believers in God; because only that way can he be considered by them as the messenger chosen by the Supreme God whom he himself has created. If you take a good look at the list of items Moses got from the leaders of the twelve tribes on the occasion of the dedication of the renewed tabernacle, you will see the terrific benefits and understand why it's so important to Moses. You can also see how Moses makes the most of everything he knows about the desert, by which I mean any detail which he can present as a magical and divine event, attributing it immediately to God and to his own connection with God.

11:16-22

[16] So theLord said to Moses: "Gather to Me seventy men of the elders of Israel, whom you know to be the elders of the people and officers over them; bring them to the tabernacle of meeting, that they may stand there with you.[17] Then I will come down and talk with you there. I will take of the Spirit that is upon you and will put the same upon them; and they shall bear the burden of the people with you, that you may not

bear it yourself alone. **18** Then you shall say to the people, 'Consecrate yourselves for tomorrow, and you shall eat meat; for you have wept in the hearing of the Lord, saying, "Who will give us meat to eat? For it was well with us in Egypt." Therefore the Lord will give you meat, and you shall eat. **19** You shall eat, not one day, nor two days, nor five days, nor ten days, nor twenty days, **20** but for a whole month, until it comes out of your nostrils and becomes loathsome to you, because you have despised the Lord who is among you, and have wept before Him, saying, "Why did we ever come up out of Egypt?".'"

21 And Moses said, "The people whom I am among are six hundred thousand men on foot; yet You have said, 'I will give them meat, that they may eat for a whole month.' **22** Shall flocks and herds be slaughtered for them, to provide enough for them? Or shall all the fish of the sea be gathered together for them, to provide enough for them?"

This trick of gathering seventy men from among the elders is used by Moses several times. But why are these 'policemen' needed? Their function is to convince the people that Moses is doing the right thing; and they have to spread the purported word of God and persuade the people. As for the promise that they shall have meat to eat for a whole month, until they are sick of it, it can be traced to Moses's knowledge of the desert: He knew about the quail migration from the cold North to the desert at this time of year. He knew their exact first landing spot, where they arrive en masse, totally exhausted, so that it's no effort to pick them up from the ground. Moses knew about quail migration when he was still in Egypt, through which the birds passed on their way.

11:30-33

30 And Moses returned to the camp, he and the elders of Israel. **31** Now a wind went out from the Lord, and it brought quail from the sea and left them fluttering near the camp, about a day's journey on this side and about a day's journey on the other side, all around the camp, and about two cubits above the surface of the ground. [32] And the people stayed up all that day, all night, and all the next day, and gathered the quail (he who gathered least gathered ten homers); and they spread them out for themselves all around the camp. [33] But while the meat was still between their teeth, before it was chewed, the wrath of the was aroused against the people, and the struck the people with a very great plague.

Moses uses the people's gluttony and mad rush for the free meat as an excuse to satisfy his lust for mass murder, masking it as anger at their supposed lack of faith in God, then records it in his book as a murder perpetrated by God.

13:1-3

[1] And the spoke to Moses, saying, [2] "Send men to spy out the land of Canaan, which I am giving to the children of Israel; from each tribe of their fathers you shall send a man, every one a leader among them."
[3] So Moses sent them from the Wilderness of Paran according to the command of the , all of them men who were heads of the children of Israel.

13:17-25

[17] Then Moses sent them to spy out the land of Canaan, and said to them, "Go up this way into the South, and go up to the mountains, [18] and see what the land is like: whether the people who dwell in it are strong or weak, few or many; [19] whether the land they dwell in is good or bad; whether the cities they inhabit are like camps or strongholds; [20] whether the land is rich or poor; and whether there are forests there or not. Be of good courage. And bring some of the fruit of the land." Now the time was the season of the first ripe grapes.
[21] So they went up and spied out the land from the Wilderness of Zin as far as Rehob, near the entrance of Hamath. [22] And they went up through the South and came to

Hebron; Ahiman, Sheshai, and Talmai, the descendants of Anak, were there. (Now Hebron was built seven years before Zoan in Egypt.) [23] Then they came to the Valley of Eshcol, and there cut down a branch with one cluster of grapes; they carried it between two of them on a pole. They also brought some of the pomegranates and figs. [24] The place was called the Valley of Eshcol,[c] because of the cluster which the men of Israel cut down there. [25] And they returned from spying out the land after forty days.

13:26 -14:4

[26] Now they departed and came back to Moses and Aaron and all the congregation of the children of Israel in the Wilderness of Paran, at Kadesh; they brought back word to them and to all the congregation, and showed them the fruit of the land. [27] Then they told him, and said: "We went to the land where you sent us. It truly flows with milk and honey, and this is its fruit.[28] Nevertheless the people who dwell in the land are strong; the cities are fortified and very large; moreover we saw the descendants of Anak there.[29] The Amalekites dwell in the land of the South; the Hittites, the Jebusites, and the Amorites dwell in the mountains; and the Canaanites dwell by the sea and along the banks of the Jordan."

[30] Then Caleb quieted the people before Moses, and said, "Let us go up at once and take possession, for we are well able to overcome it."

[31] But the men who had gone up with him said, "We are not able to go up against the people, for they are stronger than we." [32] And they gave the children of Israel a bad report of the land which they had spied out, saying, "The land through which we have gone as spies is a land that devours its inhabitants, and all the people whom we saw in it are men of great stature. [33] There we saw the giants[d] (the descendants of Anak came from the giants); and we were like grasshoppers in our own sight, and so we were in their sight."

[14] So all the congregation lifted up their voices and cried, and the people wept that night. [2] And all the children of Israel

complained against Moses and Aaron, and the whole congregation said to them, "If only we had died in the land of Egypt! Or if only we had died in this wilderness! ³ Why has the Lord brought us to this land to fall by the sword, that our wives and children should become victims? Would it not be better for us to return to Egypt?" ⁴ So they said to one another, "Let us select a leader and return to Egypt."

The information brought back by the spies after touring the land, particularly the description of the giants living there, compared to whom the spies seemed like grasshoppers, causes dejection among the people, who want to go back to Egypt and live there as slaves. When reading the people's complaints against Moses, one can see that a massacre is imminent.

14:5-10

⁵ Then Moses and Aaron fell on their faces before all the assembly of the congregation of the children of Israel.

⁶ But Joshua the son of Nun and Caleb the son of Jephunneh, who were among those who had spied out the land, tore their clothes; ⁷ and they spoke to all the congregation of the children of Israel, saying: "The land we passed through to spy out is an exceedingly good land. ⁸ If the Lord delights in us, then He will bring us into this land and give it to us, 'a land which flows with milk and honey.'[a] ⁹ Only do not rebel against the Lord, nor fear the people of the land, for they are our bread; their protection has departed from them, and the Lord is with us. Do not fear them."

¹⁰ And all the congregation said to stone them with stones. Now the glory of the Lord appeared in the tabernacle of meeting before all the children of Israel.

Joshua son of Nun and Caleb son of Jephunneh try to calm down and encourage the people, but the community won't calm down, to the extent of wanting to stone them to death. Even the appearance of the pillar of smoke apparently no longer has a soothing effect on them.

14:11-20

¹¹ Then the Lord said to Moses: "How long will these people reject Me? And how long will they not believe Me, with all the signs which I have performed among them? ¹² I will strike them with the pestilence and disinherit them, and I will make of you a nation greater and mightier than they."

¹³ And Moses said to the Lord: "Then the Egyptians will hear it, for by Your might You brought these people up from among them, ¹⁴ and they will tell it to the inhabitants of this land. They have heard that You, Lord, are among these people; that You, Lord, are seen face to face and Your cloud stands above them, and You go before them in a pillar of cloud by day and in a pillar of fire by night. ¹⁵ Now if You kill these people as one man, then the nations which have heard of Your fame will speak, saying, ¹⁶ 'Because the Lord was not able to bring this people to the land which He swore to give them, therefore He killed them in the wilderness.' ¹⁷ And now, I pray, let the power of my Lord be great, just as You have spoken, saying, ¹⁸ 'The Lord is longsuffering and abundant in mercy, forgiving iniquity and transgression; but He by no means clears the guilty, visiting the iniquity of the fathers on the children to the third and fourth generation.'[b] ¹⁹ Pardon the iniquity of this people, I pray, according to the greatness of Your mercy, just as You have forgiven this people, from Egypt even until now."

²⁰ Then the Lord said: "I have pardoned, according to your word."

Once again the Lord speaks to Moses, telling him he'd like to wipe out the entire congregation and make Moses (and his descendants, presumably) into a great nation. But Moses mollifies God, using a version of the 'what will the neighbors say?' argument, and gets God to forgive the people of Israel. The interesting point here is, that God was apparently willing to strike the entire people down with the plague; in my opinion, he'd have done better to inflict the plague on all the people living at the time in the Promised Land, and then walk his people into the land of milk and honey, as he had promised, a land that had been cleansed of its inhabitants. But who am I to advise God. This may be the place to recall that Moses was quite the expert at spreading the plague, already at the time he appeared before Pharaoh in Egypt, during the 'Let my people go' story.

About five hundred years ago a terrible case of the plague spread through Europe, killing some 75 million people, which at the time constituted half of the continent's population. At least we know that Moses wasn't involved, even if Mel Gibson may have thought otherwise.

14:21-25

[21] "But truly, as I live, all the earth shall be filled with the glory of the Lord— [22] because all these men who have seen My glory and the signs which I did in Egypt and in the wilderness, and have put Me to the test now these ten times, and have not heeded My voice,[23] they certainly shall not see the land of which I swore to their fathers, nor shall any of those who rejected Me see it. [24] But My servant Caleb, because he has a different spirit in him and has followed Me fully, I will bring into the land where he went, and his descendants shall inherit it.[25] Now the Amalekites and the Canaanites dwell in the valley; tomorrow turn and move out into the wilderness by the Way of the Red Sea."

God is angry at all the people who don't see that His Glory fills the entire country – according to Moses, of course – nor do they respect all the signs that He sent to Pharoah, via Moses, who supposedly learnt those tricks from God; nor all the tests that supposedly the people of Israel tested God and which, for some reason, we've never heard of to this very day. So is God also mad at those who didn't see nor heed all the signs that God sent them, including the pillar of smoke in daytime and the pillar of fire at night; yet there are apparently many who simply don't believe all these miracles and wonders, considering them as mere trickery.

14:26-35

[26] And the Lord spoke to Moses and Aaron, saying, [27] "How long shall I bear with this evil congregation who complain against Me? I have heard the complaints which the children of Israel make against Me. [28] Say to them, 'As I live,' says the Lord, 'just as you have spoken in My hearing, so I will do to you: [29] The carcasses of you who have complained against Me shall fall in this wilderness, all of you who were numbered, according to your entire number, from twenty years old and above. [30] Except for Caleb the son of Jephunneh and Joshua the son of Nun, you shall by no means enter the land which I swore I would make you dwell in. [31] But your little ones, whom you said would be victims, I will bring in, and they shall know the land which you have despised. [32] But as for you, your carcasses shall fall in this wilderness. [33] And your sons shall be shepherds in the wilderness forty years, and bear the brunt of your infidelity, until your carcasses are consumed in the wilderness. [34] According to the number of the days in which you spied out the land, forty days, for each day you shall bear your guilt one year, namely forty years, and you shall know My rejection. [35] I the Lord have spoken this. I will surely do so to all this evil congregation who are gathered together against Me. In this wilderness they shall be consumed, and there they shall die.'"

Moses is furious with the entire Israelite congregation, and as punishment he delays the continued journey to the Promised Land by forty years, one year for every day that the spies toured the country; and this because the people preferred to go back to slavery in Egypt rather than try to conquer the land. Therefore, Moses promises the people that all those who left Egypt shall die in the desert, and their carcasses shall remain in the desert. Moses's intention is to replace the generation of slaves with a new, born-free generation; a generation of proud men who never experienced the humiliation of being slaves.

14:36

[36] Now the men whom Moses sent to spy out the land, who returned and made all the congregation complain against him by bringing a bad report of the land, [37] those very men who brought the evil report about the land, died by the plague before the Lord. [38] But Joshua the son of Nun and Caleb the son of Jephunneh remained alive, of the men who went to spy out the land.

Moses knows full well that the people's army is not ready for war at this point; yet he won't resist the opportunity for a massacre, albeit a small one, and so he gets rid of all the spies who told the congregation things Moses didn't want them to say. His method of killing this time is of a type he calls a plague, the implementation of which he of course assigns to God. Let's keep in mind that the spies were supposedly chosen by God, and they were among the leaders of the Israelites.

13:3

[3] So Moses sent them from the Wilderness of Paran according to the command of the Lord, all of them men who were heads of the children of Israel.

Is it possible that Moses simply decided to replace the leadership? If so, he did it in his favorite fashion.

14:39-45

[39] Then Moses told these words to all the children of Israel, and the people mourned greatly. [40] And they rose early in the morning and went up to the top of the mountain, saying, "Here we are, and we will go up to the place which the Lord has promised, for we have sinned!"

⁴¹ And Moses said, "Now why do you transgress the command of the Lord? For this will not succeed. ⁴² Do not go up, lest you be defeated by your enemies, for the Lord is not among you. ⁴³ For the Amalekites and the Canaanites are there before you, and you shall fall by the sword; because you have turned away from the Lord, the Lord will not be with you."

⁴⁴ But they presumed to go up to the mountaintop. Nevertheless, neither the ark of the covenant of the Lord nor Moses departed from the camp. ⁴⁵ Then the Amalekites and the Canaanites who dwelt in that mountain came down and attacked them, and drove them back as far as Hormah.

This is an example of the possible outcomes of religious extremism. Moses's accusations caused some of the people – the more religiously extreme – to run up the mountain, in the belief that the Lord would be there for them, guide them how to overcome the enemy which God had promised to vanquish, thus rescuing them in their hour of need. Or perhaps it was the fear that God would kill them in a plague, that spurred them to run up the mountain and die there on their swords. But reality and the truth are far crueler, more lethal and tragic, in such cases.

15:1-7

¹ And the Lord spoke to Moses, saying,² "Speak to the children of Israel, and say to them: 'When you have come into the land you are to inhabit, which I am giving to you, ³ and you make an offering by fire to the Lord, a burnt offering or a sacrifice, to fulfill a vow or as a freewill offering or in your appointed feasts, to make a sweet aroma to the Lord, from the herd or the flock, ⁴ then he who presents his offering to the Lord shall bring a grain offering of one-tenth of an ephah of fine flour mixed with one-fourth of a hin of oil; ⁵ and one-fourth of a hin of wine as a drink offering you shall prepare with the burnt offering for the sacrifice, for each lamb.⁶ Or for a ram you shall prepare as a grain offering two-tenths of an ephah of fine flour mixed with one-third of a hin of oil; ⁷ and

as a drink offering you shall offer one-third of a hin of wine as a sweet aroma to the Lord.

Moses, however, carries on with 'business as usual', focusing on how the Israelites should act upon reaching the promised land – an event scheduled for another forty years.

15:32-36

[32] Now while the children of Israel were in the wilderness, they found a man gathering sticks on the Sabbath day. [33] And those who found him gathering sticks brought him to Moses and Aaron, and to all the congregation. [34] They put him under guard, because it had not been explained what should be done to him.
[35] Then the Lord said to Moses, "The man must surely be put to death; all the congregation shall stone him with stones outside the camp." [36] So, as the Lord commanded Moses, all the congregation brought him outside the camp and stoned him with stones, and he died.

A man was caught gathering firewood on the Sabbath, and the people who caught him in the act hand him over to Moses and Aaron, and he is placed in custody because they don't know exactly what's to be done with him. Then God reads Moses's mind, knows exactly what to do, and relays the sentence to Moses. Moses and Aaron, who already knew what the sentence would be even before God, call up the entire congregation, and together they stone the wrongdoer to death. Could all this really happen on the Sabbath? Apparently, on the Sabbath it is permissible to stone practically any living thing; which is an occurrence we witness to this very day.

15:37-39

[37] Again the Lord spoke to Moses, saying, [38] "Speak to the children of Israel: Tell them to make tassels on the corners of their garments throughout their generations, and to put a blue thread in the tassels of the corners. [39] And you shall have the

tassel, that you may look upon it and remember all the commandments of the Lord and do them, and that you may not follow the harlotry to which your own heart and your own eyes are inclined,

Moses, with all his ingrained cruelty, nonetheless displays a wild sense of humor. Just imagine this idea he had, of getting the entire congregation to wear tassels. This begs the question: Does a decent man, who got a proper education, need to wear a small prayer shawl (*'talis'*) 24/7, so as not to forget to follow the commandments? If that isn't an act of scorn and contempt for human beings, then what is?

16:1-7

[1] Now Korah the son of Izhar, the son of Kohath, the son of Levi, with Dathan and Abiram the sons of Eliab, and On the son of Peleth, sons of Reuben, took men; [2] and they rose up before Moses with some of the children of Israel, two hundred and fifty leaders of the congregation, representatives of the congregation, men of renown. [3] They gathered together against Moses and Aaron, and said to them, "You take too much upon yourselves, for all the congregation is holy, every one of them, and the Lord is among them. Why then do you exalt yourselves above the assembly of the Lord?"
[4] So when Moses heard it, he fell on his face;[5] and he spoke to Korah and all his company, saying, "Tomorrow morning the Lord will show who is His and who is holy, and will cause him to come near to Him. That one whom He chooses He will cause to come near to Him. [6] Do this: Take censers, Korah and all your company; [7] put fire in them and put incense in them before the Lord tomorrow, and it shall be that the man whom the Lord chooses is the holy one. You take too much upon yourselves, you sons of Levi!"

What we feared has come to pass: a group of people challenge Moses and his governance, and denounce him for holding himself above the rest of God's chosen. When Moses hears this, he supposedly, or metaphorically, fell on his face. It is quite clear that Moses already knew of Korah and his men and their intent to rebel. Considering the means available to Moses, he probably had his own cadre of intelligence-gatherers, who were loyal to him.

16:8-11

[8] Then Moses said to Korah, "Hear now, you sons of Levi: [9] Is it a small thing to you that the God of Israel has separated you from the congregation of Israel, to bring you near to Himself, to do the work of the tabernacle of the Lord, and to stand before the congregation to serve them; [10] and that He has brought you near to Himself, you and all your brethren, the sons of Levi, with you? And are you seeking the priesthood also? [11] Therefore you and all your company are gathered together against the Lord. And what is Aaron that you complain against him?"

Moses denounced Korah and his cohorts and reminds them that, as Levis, they're in a good position, since God chose them to do tabernacle work, which already brings them close to the inner circle, the ruling elite; he is enraged with them for pointing out his lordliness.

16:12-15

[12] And Moses sent to call Dathan and Abiram the sons of Eliab, but they said, "We will not come up! [13] Is it a small thing that you have brought us up out of a land flowing with milk and honey, to kill us in the wilderness, that you should keep acting like a prince over us? [14] Moreover you have not brought us into a land flowing with milk and honey, nor given us inheritance of fields and vineyards. Will you put out the eyes of these men? We will not come up!"
[15] Then Moses was very angry, and said to the Lord, "Do not respect their offering. I have not taken one donkey from them, nor have I hurt one of them."

Moses summons Dathan and Abiram, sons of Eliab, to him but they refuse to come. They complain along the lines of: Isn't it enough that you took us away from a land of milk and honey to kill us in the desert, while you rule us? You haven't brought us to a land of milk and honey, nor have we gotten any land, field or vineyard; are you trying to deceive us?" It sounds as if Moses had persuaded many people who had lived as free men in Egypt to agree to leave Egypt with him, probably by promising to lead them to a fertile country where they would get a field and a vineyard of their own. These people weren't slaves, lived there as free men; it therefore follows that many who joined Moses's adventure actually came out as losers. Moses appeals to God, actually sounding as if he's commanding God, to reject Dathan and Abiram's offering. Moses must have known that they would not have any more chances to make sacrifices in the future.

16:16-19

[16] And Moses said to Korah, "Tomorrow, you and all your company be present before the Lord—you and they, as well as Aaron. [17] Let each take his censer and put incense in it, and each of you bring his censer before the Lord, two hundred and fifty censers; both you and Aaron, each with his censer." [18] So every man took his censer, put fire in it, laid incense on it, and stood at the door of the tabernacle of meeting with Moses and Aaron. [19] And Korah gathered all the congregation against them at the door of the tabernacle of meeting. Then the glory of the Lord appeared to all the congregation.

Moses asks Korah and his company to come to the entrance to the tabernacle with their censers, light a fire in them and place incense in it. Korah and his men fall right into the trap arranged by Moses, the pyrotechnics expert. Moses was aware of Korah's plans from the moment the latter first organized his men, so he had plenty of time to decide what to do with them, prepare the various measures until the final liquidation of Korah and all his followers. Which, to Moses, is the only solution when dealing with people's complaints towards him or towards God; or with anyone who tries to grab a portion of his achievements for which he worked so hard. But this time, it's personal: Moses was offended by the criticism and disrespect leveled at him. Also, Moses may have wanted to take advantage of this event to stop any future organized acts of disobedience, by taking out all Korah's followers, people who were better educated than the rest of the rabble.

16:20-22

[20] And the Lord spoke to Moses and Aaron, saying, [21] "Separate yourselves from among this congregation, that I may consume them in a moment."
[22] Then they fell on their faces, and said, "O God, the God of the spirits of all flesh, shall one man sin, and You be angry with all the congregation?"

God supposedly speaks to Moses and Aaron, telling them not to stand next to Korah and his company because He is going to annihilate them. Moses pretends to defend them, because of the way he records events in his book; Moses always attributes the murders he and his lackeys commit to God's will. It seems that in order to write down all the history, Moses definitely needs God; otherwise he could be accused of massacre and mass murder.

16:23-35

[23] So the Lord spoke to Moses, saying, [24] "Speak to the congregation, saying, 'Get away from the tents of Korah, Dathan and Abiram.'"
[25] Then Moses rose and went to Dathan and Abiram, and the elders of Israel followed him. [26] And he spoke to the congregation, saying, "Depart now from the tents of these wicked men! Touch nothing of theirs, lest you be consumed in

all their sins." ²⁷ So they got away from around the tents of Korah, Dathan, and Abiram; and Dathan and Abiram came out and stood at the door of their tents, with their wives, their sons, and their little children.

²⁸ And Moses said: "By this you shall know that the Lord has sent me to do all these works, for I have not done them of my own will. ²⁹ If these men die naturally like all men, or if they are visited by the common fate of all men, then the Lord has not sent me. ³⁰ But if the Lord creates a new thing, and the earth opens its mouth and swallows them up with all that belongs to them, and they go down alive into the pit, then you will understand that these men have rejected the Lord."

³¹ Now it came to pass, as he finished speaking all these words, that the ground split apart under them, ³² and the earth opened its mouth and swallowed them up, with their households and all the men with Korah, with all their goods. ³³ So they and all those with them went down alive into the pit; the earth closed over them, and they perished from among the assembly. ³⁴ Then all Israel who were around them fled at their cry, for they said, "Lest the earth swallow us up also!"

³⁵ And a fire came out from the Lord and consumed the two hundred and fifty men who were offering incense.

Briefly, God tells Moses to summon the whole congregation around the 'living quarters' of Korah and his clan, then warns the people to get away from those wicked ones and everything belonging to them, since they might die because of Korah's sins. Korah et al., having heard the commotion, step out of their tents with their kids. Moses addresses them, in the presence of the entire community, saying that God has sent him. Once again Moses transforms mass murder into a holy act committed by God, thereby also proving God's existence. Moses declares that, should the earth swallow up Korah and his clan, this is because they cursed God. Moses has already sentenced them all to death, and has prepared the landslide around Korah's home. At the right moment, at a sign given by Moses to his henchmen, the earth sinks beneath Korah's feet, and the entire clan falls into the huge hole in the ground. In keeping with his specialty, Moses completes the spectacle with a burst of fire that finished off the culprits.

Moses dragged the congregation of Israelites to the scene to watch an event supposedly done by God, presenting it as proof that God committed the murder, while at the same time getting rid of his opponents. But actually, upon reading the story, we see there is no mention of Korah having cursed God. So why does Moses make such a serious false accusation? Finally, Moses murders Korah and his clan in cold blood, complete with fire – his favorite trick. After this vile crime committed by Moses, I re-read the chapter to remind myself how it all started. And it becomes clear that, in fact, Korah and his followers did not want anything from Moses; they only denounced him for luring them with false promises to join him in his adventure. And they censured him for his haughtiness over the rest of God's servants, whom they whole-heartedly believed they were part of. But Moses misrepresented the events, to make it easier for him to eliminate them – in God's name, of course.

16:41-50

[41] On the next day all the congregation of the children of Israel complained against Moses and Aaron, saying, "You have killed the people of the Lord." [42] Now it happened, when the congregation had gathered against Moses and Aaron, that they turned toward the tabernacle of meeting; and suddenly the cloud covered it, and the glory of the Lord appeared. [43] Then Moses and Aaron came before the tabernacle of meeting.

[44] And the Lord spoke to Moses, saying, [45] "Get away from among this congregation, that I may consume them in a moment."

And they fell on their faces.

[46] So Moses said to Aaron, "Take a censer and put fire in it from the altar, put incense on it, and take it quickly to the congregation and make atonement for them; for wrath has gone out from the Lord. The plague has begun." [47] Then Aaron

took it as Moses commanded, and ran into the midst of the assembly; and already the plague had begun among the people. So he put in the incense and made atonement for the people.[48] And he stood between the dead and the living; so the plague was stopped. [49] Now those who died in the plague were fourteen thousand seven hundred, besides those who died in the Korah incident. [50] So Aaron returned to Moses at the door of the tabernacle of meeting, for the plague had stopped.

The people are not convinced by the spectacle staged by Moses, and accuse him and Aaron of murdering 'the people of the Lord', i.e. God's servants. When the congregation closes in on Moses and Aaron, the latter retreat to the tabernacle, and Moses switches on the smoke screen, or cloud. Moses apparently foresaw that the congregation may prove reluctant to accept the murder of Korah & Sons as a divine act of God, and so he prepared in advance Plan B to protect him from the rabble that might at any moment attack him. Moses instructs Aaron to take a censer with fire from the altar, sprinkle incense on it, and rush towards the protestors, seemingly to atone and protect them from God's wrath, since God has apparently attacked them with some deadly plague.

I don't see any logic in this step, supposedly aimed at telling God to stop the plague. In fact, the substance in the censer, heated together with the incense, is probably what caused anyone who inhaled it to suffocate to death. When Aaron was running with outstretched arm carrying the cesner, his mouth and nose were undoubtedly covered – a detail Moses conveniently failed to log in his book. And so Aaron ended up murdering fourteen thousand and seven hundred people, in God's name of course. Another possibility is that some of the people were served a sweet drink shortly before Aaron's rush into the crowd with the censer. No need for me to recommend the use of cyanide to Moses and Aaron; I am sure they were both familiar with various potent poisons found in nature. What this incident makes clear is that a large number of people must have surrounded the tabernacle, demanding an explanation for the slaughter of Korah and his company by Moses and Aaron.

17:1-9

¹And the Lord spoke to Moses, saying: ²"Speak to the children of Israel, and get from them a rod from each father's house, all their leaders according to their fathers' houses - twelve rods. Write each man's name on his rod. ³ And you shall write Aaron's name on the rod of Levi. For there shall be one rod for the head of each father's house. ⁴ Then you shall place them in the tabernacle of meeting before the Testimony, where I meet with you. ⁵ And it shall be that the rod of the man whom I choose will blossom; thus I will rid Myself of the complaints of the children of Israel, which they make against you."

⁶ So Moses spoke to the children of Israel, and each of their leaders gave him a rod apiece, for each leader according to their fathers' houses, twelve rods; and the rod of Aaron was among their rods. ⁷ And Moses placed the rods before the Lord in the tabernacle of witness.

⁸ Now it came to pass on the next day that Moses went into the tabernacle of witness, and behold, the rod of Aaron, of the house of Levi, had sprouted and put forth buds, had produced blossoms and yielded ripe almonds. ⁹ Then Moses brought out all the rods from before the Lord to all the children of Israel; and they looked, and each man took his rod.

Moses continues with his tricks, to prove that God chose Aaron's rod from among the rods of all the community leaders: Aaron's rod blossomed with almond buds, so he was evidently the chosen leader. Moses uses this trick to illustrate that Aaron is God's choice of a leader – though I don't see a logical connection here. Incidentally – cyanide is produced from bitter almonds.

17:10-11

[10] And the Lord said to Moses, "Bring Aaron's rod back before the Testimony, to be kept as a sign against the rebels, that you may put their complaints away from Me, lest they die." [11] Thus did Moses; just as the Lord had commanded him, so he did.

I think that after the mass murder committed by Moses and Aaron on their own people, a long time would pass before anyone dared to complain again, no matter about what. I am not sure, however, how long Moses will be able to restrain himself and overcome his appetite for killing.

17:12-13

[12] So the children of Israel spoke to Moses, saying, "Surely we die, we perish, we all perish! [13] Whoever even comes near the tabernacle of the Lord must die. Shall we all utterly die?"

The despair echoing in these verses clearly illustrates the people's feelings; they must have been on the brink of total despair: 'Shall we utterly die?' is a horrifying question, full of hopelessness.

18:1-7

[1] Then the Lord said to Aaron: "You and your sons and your father's house with you shall bear the iniquity related to the sanctuary, and you and your sons with you shall bear the iniquity associated with your priesthood. [2] Also bring with you your brethren of the tribe of Levi, the tribe of your father, that they may be joined with you and serve you while you and your sons are with you before the tabernacle of witness. [3] They shall attend to your needs and all the needs of the tabernacle; but they shall not come near the articles of the sanctuary and the altar, lest they die - they and you also. [4] They shall be joined with you and attend to the needs of the tabernacle of meeting,

for all the work of the tabernacle; but an outsider shall not come near you. [5] And you shall attend to the duties of the sanctuary and the duties of the altar, that there may be no more wrath on the children of Israel.[6] Behold, I Myself have taken your brethren the Levites from among the children of Israel; they are a gift to you, given by the Lord, to do the work of the tabernacle of meeting. [7] Therefore you and your sons with you shall attend to your priesthood for everything at the altar and behind the veil; and you shall serve. I give your priesthood to you as a gift for service, but the outsider who comes near shall be put to death."

Once again the threat of a death sentence; this time, to any who approach the tabernacle. Moses must have had something very important to hide there, which caused him to issue such irrational edicts. Could it be cutlery God used to consume the gargantuan quantities of food served to him? Think about it: Since the destruction of the Second Temple, the practice of sacrifices to God was discontinued. Add to that the fact that God was used to consuming huge quantities of the stuff, then suddenly the supply runs dry; this must be what caused God to starve to death. There is no doubt in my mind that, had God been vegetarian, as he was supposed to be, we would still be seeing Him amongst us to this very day, as we always did.

18:8-20

[8] And the Lord spoke to Aaron: "Here, I Myself have also given you charge of My heave offerings, all the holy gifts of the children of Israel; I have given them as a portion to you and your sons, as an ordinance forever. [9] This shall be yours of the most holy things reserved from the fire: every offering of theirs, every grain offering and every sin offering and every trespass offering which they render to Me, shall be most holy for you and your sons. [10] In a most holy place you shall eat it; every male shall eat it. It shall be holy to you.

[11] "This also is yours: the heave offering of their gift, with all the wave offerings of the children of Israel; I have given

them to you, and your sons and daughters with you, as an ordinance forever. Everyone who is clean in your house may eat it.

[12] "All the best of the oil, all the best of the new wine and the grain, their firstfruits which they offer to the Lord, I have given them to you. [13] Whatever first ripe fruit is in their land, which they bring to the Lord, shall be yours. Everyone who is clean in your house may eat it.

[14] "Every devoted thing in Israel shall be yours.

[15] "Everything that first opens the womb of all flesh, which they bring to the Lord, whether man or beast, shall be yours; nevertheless the firstborn of man you shall surely redeem, and the firstborn of unclean animals you shall redeem. [16] And those redeemed of the devoted things you shall redeem when one month old, according to your valuation, for five shekels of silver, according to the shekel of the sanctuary, which is twenty gerahs. [17] But the firstborn of a cow, the firstborn of a sheep, or the firstborn of a goat you shall not redeem; they are holy. You shall sprinkle their blood on the altar, and burn their fat as an offering made by fire for a sweet aroma to the Lord. [18] And their flesh shall be yours, just as the wave breast and the right thigh are yours.

[19] "All the heave offerings of the holy things, which the children of Israel offer to the Lord, I have given to you and your sons and daughters with you as an ordinance forever; it is a covenant of salt forever before the Lord with you and your descendants with you."

[20] Then the Lord said to Aaron: "You shall have no inheritance in their land, nor shall you have any portion among them; I am your portion and your inheritance among the children of Israel."

This time, God addresses Aaron only, and dictates to him his share in the will, promising Aaron and his offspring forevermore all the sacrifices, gifts and penalties that the Israelites will pay God at the tabernacle. Apparently, Aaron felt that he was approaching the end of his days, and so he makes arrangements for taking care of his progeny's welfare for all eternity. I do wonder, though, how come Moses and Aaron were so sure, at the time, that the belief in God would be world-wide and would persist for so long; and that no one would discover the truth. However, many different groups did arise, who joined and further expanded the tenets of this faith in a variety of ways. And of course there's nothing to prevent more groups and cults from forming, who will preserve and further develop the belief in God; despite the detailed and important information presented here.

18:21-24

[21] "Behold, I have given the children of Levi all the tithes in Israel as an inheritance in return for the work which they perform, the work of the tabernacle of meeting. [22] Hereafter the children of Israel shall not come near the tabernacle of meeting, lest they bear sin and die. [23] But the Levites shall perform the work of the tabernacle of meeting, and they shall bear their iniquity; it shall be a statute forever, throughout your generations, that among the children of Israel they shall have no inheritance. [24] For the tithes of the children of Israel, which they offer up as a heave offering to the Lord, I have given to the Levites as an inheritance; therefore I have said to them, 'Among the children of Israel they shall have no inheritance.'"

The tribe of Levi is also written up in God's will: As they have served God in the tabernacle so loyally, God is passing on to them all the tithes, offerings and gifts that God receives from all the people of Israel. Usually, the writer of a will is a person of advanced age, who wishes that his loved ones inherit his assets upon his death. But here we see that Aaron is the one about to die, and he wills all of God's assets to his own family and descendents forever. It sounds strange, but not terrible. There is some logic to it: After all, it was Moses and Aaron who reinvented God, polishing and fine-tuning their invention to the highest degree. So they and their offspring are eligible to get all present and future royalties to be gained from this wonderful invention, forever and ever.

19:1-10

[1] Now the Lord spoke to Moses and Aaron, saying, [2] "This is the ordinance of the law which the Lord has commanded, saying: 'Speak to the children of Israel, that they bring you a red heifer without blemish, in which there is no defect and on which a yoke has never come. [3] You shall give it to Eleazar the priest, that he may take it outside the camp, and it shall be slaughtered before him; [4] and Eleazar the priest shall take some of its blood with his finger, and sprinkle some of its blood seven times directly in front of the tabernacle of meeting. [5] Then the heifer shall be burned in his sight: its hide, its flesh, its blood, and its offal shall be burned. [6] And the priest shall take cedar wood and hyssop and scarlet, and cast them into the midst of the fire burning the heifer. [7] Then the priest shall wash his clothes, he shall bathe in water, and afterward he shall come into the camp; the priest shall be unclean until evening. [8] And the one who burns it shall wash his clothes in water, bathe in water, and shall be unclean until evening. [9] Then a man who is clean shall gather up the ashes of the heifer, and store them outside the camp in a clean place; and they shall be kept for the congregation of the children of Israel for the water of purification; it is for purifying from sin. [10] And the one who gathers the ashes of the heifer shall wash his clothes, and be unclean until evening. It shall be a statute forever to the children of Israel and to the stranger who dwells among them.'"

This is a detailed explanation of how to carry out a distinctly pagan ritual. First, you need a young red cow, totally blemish-free, which has not yet been used for labor. The cow is given to the high priest, who must slaughter it outside the camp, then dip his finger in its blood. The text doesn't state which finger, but the index finger of the right hand seems a good choice, since it is used to indicate any direction. Then the priest must splash the blood seven times in the direction of the temple, or the chief house of worship where he lives. Then burn the cow – flesh, hide, blood, entrails and all – while adding cedar wood and hyssop, and most importantly some aphids (or bits of scarlet produced from these insects.) Once he's cleansed, the pure man must then collect the ashes and place them outside the camp, in a clean place, keeping it there for the community for purification purposes, such as for women after menstruation. According to the text, there's no need for an audience during the burning, it's enough to have the high priest; he's the one who burns the cow; and being a pure man he also qualifies to collect the ashes and put them in a clean place.

The entire story reflects Moses's unique sarcasm and sense of humor. This seems to be but another of his techniques by which to collect meat from his flock. It sounds somewhat like a bet between Moses and one of his entourage, in which Moses proves that he can still find ways of procuring grilled meat for his nearest and dearest, ways that will be gladly accepted by his believers. Moses is not bothered by the fact that the ritual might seem weird, and I totally understand him.

20:1-6

[1] Then the children of Israel, the whole congregation, came into the Wilderness of Zin in the first month, and the people stayed in Kadesh; and Miriam died there and was buried there.

[2] Now there was no water for the congregation; so they gathered together against Moses and Aaron. [3] And the people contended with Moses and spoke, saying: "If only we had died when our brethren died before the Lord! [4] Why have you brought up the assembly of the Lord into this wilderness, that we and our animals should die here? [5] And why have you made us come up out of Egypt, to bring us to this evil place? It is not a place of grain or figs or vines or pomegranates; nor is there any water to drink." [6] So Moses and Aaron went from the presence of the assembly to the door of the tabernacle of meeting, and they fell on their faces. And the glory of the Lord appeared to them.

Moses and Aaron initiate a small rebellion, which enables them once again to illustrate the wonders of the Lord, by solving the water shortage that had come about.

20:7-11

⁷ Then the Lord spoke to Moses, saying, ⁸ "Take the rod; you and your brother Aaron gather the congregation together. Speak to the rock before their eyes, and it will yield its water; thus you shall bring water for them out of the rock, and give drink to the congregation and their animals."⁹ So Moses took the rod from before the Lord as He commanded him.

¹⁰ And Moses and Aaron gathered the assembly together before the rock; and he said to them, "Hear now, you rebels! Must we bring water for you out of this rock?" ¹¹ Then Moses lifted his hand and struck the rock twice with his rod; and water came out abundantly, and the congregation and their animals drank.

Moses, who had trekked through the desert extensively with Jethro's flock in search of grazing land, must have passed by the location of this particular spring countless times. But Moses, being an educated man, understood that it would be wise to plug up the hole whence the water flowed, for future use. As an amateur stonemason, he prepared some kind of plug and plugged up the hole. Now, when there's demand for water, Moses leads his congregation toward this spring. Here he can again use his knowledge to create a divine event, which will strengthen the faith of the believers and possibly add new believers. The mere fact that he had to strike the rock twice with his rod indicates that Moses had done a good job of plugging it up in the past.

20:14-21

¹⁴ Now Moses sent messengers from Kadesh to the king of Edom. "Thus says your brother Israel: 'You know all the hardship that has befallen us, ¹⁵ how our fathers went down to

Egypt, and we dwelt in Egypt a long time, and the Egyptians afflicted us and our fathers. [16] When we cried out to the LORD, He heard our voice and sent the Angel and brought us up out of Egypt; now here we are in Kadesh, a city on the edge of your border. [17] Please let us pass through your country. We will not pass through fields or vineyards, nor will we drink water from wells; we will go along the King's Highway; we will not turn aside to the right hand or to the left until we have passed through your territory.'"

[18] Then Edom said to him, "You shall not pass through my land, lest I come out against you with the sword."

[19] So the children of Israel said to him, "We will go by the Highway, and if I or my livestock drink any of your water, then I will pay for it; let me only pass through on foot, nothing more."

[20] Then he said, "You shall not pass through." So Edom came out against them with many men and with a strong hand. [21] Thus Edom refused to give Israel passage through his territory; so Israel turned away from him.

Apparently, Moses has forgotten God's promise to give him the land that yields milk and honey, so he grovels in front of the king of Edom, asking only to walk along the edges of his territory, promising to neither trample fields nor pass through vineyards nor use water from their wells. But the king of Edom turns him down and threatens to confront them with drawn swords.

21:1-3

The king of Arad, the Canaanite, who dwelt in the South, heard that Israel was coming on the road to Atharim. Then he fought against Israel and took some of them prisoners. [2] So Israel made a vow to the LORD, and said, "If You will indeed deliver this people into my hand, then I will utterly destroy their cities." [3] And the LORD listened to the voice of Israel and delivered up the Canaanites, and they utterly destroyed them and their cities. So the name of that place was called Hormah.

The king of Arad, located in the Negev, hears that Moses and his people are passing through his territory, and immediately comes out to fight the trespassers and takes a few prisoners. But it sounds as if Arad's realm was small and weak, because Moses decides to attack him and take over his lands. And naturally, this is a good chance for Moses to prove to the people that he is still the messenger of God Almighty; so he prays and vows that if the Lord hands the Israelites a victory over the king of Arad and his men, Moses will destroy their cities. Well, what else could Moses expect after vanquishing the king of Arad. Let's not forget that Moses left Egypt with six hundred thousand armed men.

21:4-9

[4] Then they journeyed from Mount Hor by the Way of the Red Sea, to go around the land of Edom; and the soul of the people became very discouraged on the way. [5] And the people spoke against God and against Moses: "Why have you brought us up out of Egypt to die in the wilderness? For there is no food and no water, and our soul loathes this worthless bread." [6] So the LORD sent fiery serpents among the people, and they bit the people; and many of the people of Israel died.

[7] Therefore the people came to Moses, and said, "We have sinned, for we have spoken against the LORD and against you; pray to the LORD that He take away the serpents from us." So Moses prayed for the people.

[8] Then the LORD said to Moses, "Make a fiery serpent, and set it on a pole; and it shall be that everyone who is bitten, when he looks at it, shall live." [9] So Moses made a bronze serpent, and put it on a pole; and so it was, if a serpent had bitten anyone, when he looked at the bronze serpent, he lived.

Once again the people complain against God and against Moses, and by now we know that this is a sign that another massacre is imminent. This time, Moses arranges an attack of snakes. This might be another attempt on Moses's part to reinforce belief in God. And indeed, the people turn to Moses, asking him to pray to God to remove this awful curse. Moses obliges, of course, and God for once dodges one of the ten commandments, "You shall not make for yourself a carved image, or any likeness of anything", and instructs Moses to make a copper statue (mistakenly translated as bronze in the English version of the bible) of a snake. Anyone bitten by a snake need only look at the copper snake, and they will stay alive. It could be that Moses, wanting to instill the fear of God in the people, let loose non-venomous snakes among his people. But to most humans, a snake is a snake, they are all equally scary and seem equally dangerous.

21:21-26

[21] Then Israel sent messengers to Sihon, king of the Amorites, saying, [22] "Let me pass through your land. We will not turn aside into fields or vineyards; we will not drink water from wells. We will go by the King's Highway until we have passed through your territory." [23] But Sihon would not allow Israel to pass through his territory. So Sihon gathered all his people together and went out against Israel in the wilderness, and he came to Jahaz and fought against Israel. [24] Then Israel defeated him with the edge of the sword, and took possession of his land from the Arnon to the Jabbok, as far as the people of Ammon; for the border of the people of Ammon was fortified. [25] So Israel took all these cities, and Israel dwelt in all the cities of the Amorites, in Heshbon and in all its villages. [26] For Heshbon was the city of Sihon king, of the Amorites, who had fought against the former king of Moab, and had taken all his land from his hand as far as the Arnon.

Here we see that after going through some battles, the Israelites gained experience as a fighting army, and from here on the way is open for them to conquer the land. Indeed, Sihon, king of the Amorties, loses the battle, his territory conquered by the army of Israelites. It could be that Moses's attempts to go through the territory of Sihon and the Amorites, the Canaanites, Arad and Edom, were raids intended to let the Israelite army gain battlefield experience and become brave warriors. This is the best way to train an army, making it a well-trained conquering army. True, this type of training involves many victims, but Moses was never averse to sacrificing men in order to reach his goals.

21:32-35

[32] Then Moses sent to spy out Jazer; and they took its villages and drove out the Amorites who *were* there.
[33] And they turned and went up by the way to Bashan. So Og, king of Bashan, went out against them, he and all his people, to battle at Edrei. [34] Then the LORD said to Moses, "Do not fear him, for I have delivered him into your hand, with all his people and his land; and you shall do to him as you did to Sihon, king of the Amorites, who dwelt at Heshbon." [35] So they defeated him, his sons, and all his people, until there was no survivor left him; and they took possession of his land.

This time, it's an actual war, an entire people rises to defend its country against invaders, which happen to be the Israelites. Moses, as God's representative, cheers on his army; encouragement of this sort boosts armies' morale everywhere in the world to this very day. But the Israelite army hardly needs encouragement at this stage. Some of them are already happily settled, '…every man under his vine and under his fig-tree', as a result of the previous wars. So by this time, seeing the results of their wars, every warrior was ready to take the place of the enemy and settle down on his lands.

22:2-14

[2] Now Balak the son of Zippor saw all that Israel had done to the Amorites. [3] And Moab was exceedingly afraid of the people because they were many, and Moab was sick with dread because of the children of Israel. [4] So Moab said to the elders of Midian, "Now this company will lick up everything

around us, as an ox licks up the grass of the field." And Balak the son of Zippor was king of the Moabites at that time. [5] Then he sent messengers to Balaam the son of Beor at Pethor, which is near the River in the land of the sons of his people, to call him, saying: "Look, a people has come from Egypt. See, they cover the face of the earth, and are settling next to me! [6] Therefore please come at once, curse this people for me, for they are too mighty for me. Perhaps I shall be able to defeat them and drive them out of the land, for I know that he whom you bless is blessed, and he whom you curse is cursed."

[7] So the elders of Moab and the elders of Midian departed with the diviner's fee in their hand, and they came to Balaam and spoke to him the words of Balak. [8] And he said to them, "Lodge here tonight, and I will bring back word to you, as the LORD speaks to me." So the princes of Moab stayed with Balaam.

[9] Then God came to Balaam and said, "Who are these men with you?"

[10] So Balaam said to God, "Balak the son of Zippor, king of Moab, has sent to me, saying, [11] 'Look, a people has come out of Egypt, and they cover the face of the earth. Come now, curse them for me; perhaps I shall be able to overpower them and drive them out.'"

[12] And God said to Balaam, "You shall not go with them; you shall not curse the people, for they are blessed."

[13] So Balaam rose in the morning and said to the princes of Balak, "Go back to your land, for the LORD has refused to give me permission to go with you."

[14] And the princes of Moab rose and went to Balak, and said, "Balaam refuses to come with us."

Balaam son of Beor was known throughout Moab as having special powers: those whom he blesses are blessed, and those whom he curses are cursed. So the king of Moab sends a delegation of elders to ask Balaam to come to him and help him curse this people which has come from Egypt, has taken over the land and is currently camped right opposite the Moab kingdom. Balaam was famous for being far wiser than most, and Balak king of Moab was of the opinion that he could plead with Jehova, known as the God of the Israelites, to remove this threat of the horde of Israelites along his borders; and even give him advice how to defeat them. However, once Balaam recovers from his surprise, he asks the messengers to stay overnight, saying he'll give them his answer after God communicates with him. Then God, who must have been sitting pretty close to Balaam, asks him who these people are. After Balaam updates the Lord with recent developments, God orders Balaam to neither help Balak king of Moab nor curse the people of Israel, as they are blessed. I note that Balaam apparently was not aware of Moses's recent amendments: first, that anyone who sees God will die immediately; and second, that God's form has changed to a pillar of smoke by day and a pillar of fire by night.

22:15-35

[15] Then Balak again sent princes, more numerous and more honorable than they. [16] And they came to Balaam and said to him, "Thus says Balak the son of Zippor: 'Please let nothing hinder you from coming to me; [17] for I will certainly honor you greatly, and I will do whatever you say to me. Therefore please come, curse this people for me.'"

[18] Then Balaam answered and said to the servants of Balak, "Though Balak were to give me his house full of silver and gold, I could not go beyond the word of the LORD my God, to do less or more. [19] Now therefore, please, you also stay here tonight, that I may know what more the LORD will say to me."

[20] And God came to Balaam at night and said to him, "If the men come to call you, rise *and* go with them; but only the word which I speak to you—that you shall do." [21] So Balaam rose in the morning, saddled his donkey, and went with the princes of Moab.

[22] Then God's anger was aroused because he went, and the Angel of the LORD took his stand in the way as an adversary against him. And he was riding on his donkey, and his two servants *were* with him. [23] Now the donkey saw the Angel of

the LORD standing in the way with his drawn sword in His hand, and the donkey turned aside out of the way and went into the field. So Balaam struck the donkey to turn her back onto the road. ²⁴ Then the Angel of the LORD stood in a narrow path between the vineyards, *with* a wall on this side and a wall on that side. ²⁵ And when the donkey saw the Angel of the LORD, she pushed herself against the wall and crushed Balaam's foot against the wall; so he struck her again. ²⁶ Then the Angel of the LORD went further, and stood in a narrow place where there *was* no way to turn either to the right hand or to the left. ²⁷ And when the donkey saw the Angel of the LORD, she lay down under Balaam; so Balaam's anger was aroused, and he struck the donkey with his staff.

²⁸ Then the LORD opened the mouth of the donkey, and she said to Balaam, "What have I done to you, that you have struck me these three times?"

²⁹ And Balaam said to the donkey, "Because you have abused me. I wish there were a sword in my hand, for now I would kill you!"

³⁰ So the donkey said to Balaam, "*Am* I not your donkey on which you have ridden, ever since *I became* yours, to this day? Was I ever disposed to do this to you?"

And he said, "No."

³¹ Then the LORD opened Balaam's eyes, and he saw the Angel of the LORD standing in the way with his drawn sword in his hand; and he bowed his head and fell flat on his face. ³² And the Angel of the LORD said to him, "Why have you struck your donkey these three times? Behold, I have come out to stand against you, because *your* way is perverse before me. ³³ The donkey saw ee and turned aside from ee these three times. If she had not turned aside from me, surely I would also have killed you by now, and let her live."

³⁴ And Balaam said to the Angel of the LORD, "I have sinned, for I did not know you stood in the way against me. Now therefore, if it displeases you, I will turn back."

³⁵ Then the Angel of the LORD said to Balaam, "Go with the men, but only the word that I speak to you, that you shall speak." So Balaam went with the princes of Balak.

Balak king of Moab continues sending his delegates to Balaam, this time more distinguished ones, whose task is to persuade him to come to the palace with promises of any honor his heart desires. But Balaam, like me, knew the truth: he could not help Balak king of Moab, not even for a houseful of gold and silver, and certainly not before he communicates with God. So he asks the delegates to stay over again, and waits for his meeting with God. God appears to him at night, and tells him, 'If the men come to call you, rise *and* go with them; but only the word which I speak to you—that you shall do'. Seems that God has changed his mind, and lets Balaam go to meet Balak king of Moab; but he reminds him to do only as He says. So Balaam saddles his ass and off they go. However, God gets angry with Balaam for agreeing to go with Balak's men, and this is where the incident with Balaam's ass is recounted: God's angel appearing before the ass, then opening its mouth to speak; Balaam's wish to turn around and go home; and God's command that Balaam go with the Moab officials but speak only what the Lord tells him to. I've made a point of focusing on this story because of its uniqueness, and God's obvious difficulty in deciding on the right way to act.

22:36-41

[36] Now when Balak heard that Balaam was coming, he went out to meet him at the city of Moab, which *is* on the border at the Arnon, the boundary of the territory. [37] Then Balak said to Balaam, "Did I not earnestly send to you, calling for you? Why did you not come to me? Am I not able to honor you?"
[38] And Balaam said to Balak, "Look, I have come to you! Now, have I any power at all to say anything? The word that God puts in my mouth, that I must speak." [39] So Balaam went with Balak, and they came to Kirjath Huzoth. [40] Then Balak offered oxen and sheep, and he sent *some* to Balaam and to the princes who *were* with him.

⁴¹ So it was, the next day, that Balak took Balaam and brought him up to the high places of Baal, that from there he might observe the extent of the people.

This story is proof that making sacrifices to the gods was customary with many nations that lived in that region. I don't know whether the other gods also loved meat, or whether in their case, too, it was the priests and their ilk who were meat lovers. Early on in their meeting, Balak king of Moab takes Balaam to a high place where the altar to his god, Baal, was located. At the time, if you wanted to contact your god, you had to appease him first by making a sacrifice. Since Balaam was known in the region as a person who respects and believes in the Israelites' god, Jehovah, Balak invites Balaam over, hoping the latter could plead with Jehova to remove the threat posed to his country by the Israelite army. We see that Balaam is indeed well-connected to Jehovah, because He appears to Balaam every night and advises him how to handle Balak, king of Moab.

23:1-17

¹ Then Balaam said to Balak, "Build seven altars for me here, and prepare for me here seven bulls and seven rams."
² And Balak did just as Balaam had spoken, and Balak and Balaam offered a bull and a ram on each altar. ³ Then Balaam said to Balak, "Stand by your burnt offering, and I will go; perhaps the LORD will come to meet me, and whatever He shows me I will tell you." So he went to a desolate height. ⁴ And God met Balaam, and he said to Him, "I have prepared the seven altars, and I have offered on each altar a bull and a ram."
⁵ Then the LORD put a word in Balaam's mouth, and said, "Return to Balak, and thus you shall speak." ⁶ So he returned to him, and there he was, standing by his burnt offering, he and all the princes of Moab.

⁷ And he took up his oracle and said: "Balak the king of Moab has brought me from Aram, from the mountains of the east. 'Come, curse Jacob for me, and come, denounce Israel!'
⁸ "How shall I curse whom God has not cursed? And how shall I denounce whom the LORD has not denounced? ⁹ For from the top of the rocks I see him, and from the hills I behold him; There! A people dwelling alone, not reckoning itself among the nations.
¹⁰ "Who can count the dust of Jacob, or number one-fourth of Israel? Let me die the death of the righteous, and let my end be like his!"
¹¹ Then Balak said to Balaam, "What have you done to me? I took you to curse my enemies, and look, you have blessed them bountifully!"
¹² So he answered and said, "Must I not take heed to speak what the LORD has put in my mouth?"
¹³ Then Balak said to him, "Please come with me to another place from which you may see them; you shall see only the outer part of them, and shall not see them all; curse them for me from there." ¹⁴ So he brought him to the field of Zophim, to the top of Pisgah, and built seven altars, and offered a bull and a ram on each altar.
¹⁵ And he said to Balak, "Stand here by your burnt offering while I meet the LORD over there."
¹⁶ Then the LORD met Balaam, and put a word in his mouth, and said, "Go back to Balak, and thus you shall speak."
¹⁷ So he came to him, and there he was, standing by his burnt offering, and the princes of Moab were with him. And Balak said to him, "What has the LORD spoken?"

Balaam, having met Balak king of Moab, joins him in the ritual of making a sacrifice to Baal, the god of the king of Moab. Here Balaam is inspired by God, and advises Balak to build seven altars and prepare seven bulls and seven rams. After making this sacrifice to the god Jehovah together, Balaam asks Balak to wait for him by the altars, as he's walking away, in case God wants to appear to him and say something, which he can then convey to Balak. However, God appears directly to Balak, and the latter tells Him that he has indeed set up seven altars and sacrificed a bull and a ram on each. Simultaneously, God appears also to Balaam, and tells him what to tell Balak. Balaam returns to Balak, who is now standing by the altars with all his dignitaries. Balak then embarks on a poetic speech composed of parables and allegories, supposedly inspired by God:

23:18-29

[18] Then he took up his oracle and said:

"Rise up, Balak, and hear!
Listen to me, son of Zippor!
[19] "God is not a man, that He should lie,
Nor a son of man, that He should repent.
Has He said, and will He not do?
Or has He spoken, and will He not make it good?
[20] Behold, I have received a command to bless;
He has blessed, and I cannot reverse it.
[21] "He has not observed iniquity in Jacob
Nor has He seen wickedness in Israel.
The LORD his God is with him,
And the shout of a King is among them.
[22] God brings them out of Egypt;
He has strength like a wild ox.
[23] "For there is no sorcery against Jacob,
Nor any divination against Israel.
It now must be said of Jacob
And of Israel, 'Oh, what God has done!'
[24] Look, a people rises like a lioness,
And lifts itself up like a lion;
It shall not lie down until it devours the prey,
And drinks the blood of the slain."
[25] Then Balak said to Balaam, "Neither curse them at all, nor bless them at all!"
[26] So Balaam answered and said to Balak, "Did I not tell you, saying, 'All that the LORD speaks, that I must do'?"

²⁷ Then Balak said to Balaam, "Please come, I will take you to another place; perhaps it will please God that you may curse them for me from there." ²⁸ So Balak took Balaam to the top of Peor, that overlooks the wasteland. ²⁹ Then Balaam said to Balak, "Build for me here seven altars, and prepare for me here seven bulls and seven rams."

In his speech, Balaam praises and glorifies and blesses the Israelites, but Balak – who summoned Balaam to curse them – complains about this. Balaam replies that he can only do what God tells him to. Balak doesn't give up, and proposes to take Balaam to a different vantage point, from which he can see the desert, and perhaps from there he'll be able to curse the Israelites. Balaam doesn't lose his cool and once again requests that the king build seven altars and prepare seven bulls and seven rams.

24 :1-25

¹ Now when Balaam saw that it pleased the LORD to bless Israel, he did not go as at other times, to seek to use sorcery, but he set his face toward the wilderness. ² And Balaam raised his eyes, and saw Israel encamped according to their tribes; and the Spirit of God came upon him.
³ Then he took up his oracle and said:
"The utterance of Balaam the son of Beor,
The utterance of the man whose eyes are opened,
⁴ The utterance of him who hears the words of God,
Who sees the vision of the Almighty,
Who falls down, with eyes wide open:
⁵ "How lovely are your tents, O Jacob!
Your dwellings, O Israel!
⁶ Like valleys that stretch out,
Like gardens by the riverside,
Like aloes planted by the LORD,
Like cedars beside the waters,
⁷ He shall pour water from his buckets,
And his seed shall be in many waters.

"His king shall be higher than Agag,
And his kingdom shall be exalted.
⁸ "God brings him out of Egypt;
He has strength like a wild ox;
He shall consume the nations, his enemies;
He shall break their bones
And pierce them with his arrows.
⁹ 'He bows down, he lies down as a lion;
And as a lion, who shall rouse him?'
"Blessed is he who blesses you,
And cursed is he who curses you."

¹⁰ Then Balak's anger was aroused against Balaam, and he struck his hands together; and Balak said to Balaam, "I called you to curse my enemies, and look, you have bountifully blessed them these three times! ¹¹ Now therefore, flee to your place. I said I would greatly honor you, but in fact, the LORD has kept you back from honor."

¹² So Balaam said to Balak, "Did I not also speak to your messengers whom you sent to me, saying, ¹³ 'If Balak were to give me his house full of silver and gold, I could not go beyond the word of the LORD, to do good or bad of my own will. What the LORD says, that I must speak'?¹⁴ And now, indeed, I am going to my people. Come, I will advise you what this people will do to your people in the latter days."

¹⁵ So he took up his oracle and said:
"The utterance of Balaam the son of Beor,
And the utterance of the man whose eyes are opened;
¹⁶ The utterance of him who hears the words of God,
And has the knowledge of the Most High,
Who sees the vision of the Almighty,
Who falls down, with eyes wide open:
¹⁷ "I see Him, but not now;
I behold Him, but not near;
A Star shall come out of Jacob;
A Scepter shall rise out of Israel,
And batter the brow of Moab,
And destroy all the sons of tumult.
¹⁸ "And Edom shall be a possession;

Seir also, his enemies, shall be a possession,
While Israel does valiantly.
[19] Out of Jacob One shall have dominion,
And destroy the remains of the city."
[20] Then he looked on Amalek, and he took up his oracle and said:
"Amalek was first among the nations,
But shall be last until he perishes."
[21] Then he looked on the Kenites, and he took up his oracle and said:
"Firm is your dwelling place,
And your nest is set in the rock;
[22] Nevertheless Kain shall be burned.
How long until Asshur carries you away captive?"
[23] Then he took up his oracle and said:
"Alas! Who shall live when God does this?
[24] But ships shall come from the coasts of Cyprus,
And they shall afflict Asshur and afflict Eber,
And so shall Amalek,[d] until he perishes."
[25] So Balaam rose and departed and returned to his place; Balak also went his way.

Balaam speaks, and again his poetic similes all amount to blessing the people of Israel. Balak again comments that he called upon Balaam to curse the Israelites, and instead he has now blessed them for the third time. Balaam unflinchingly reminds him that already after receiving the first invitation, he told Balak's delegates to convey to the king that even if Balak were to fill his house with gold and silver he still could say only what the Lord tells him. And so the king of Moab sends Balaam peacefully on his way, a conduct showing that the king of Moab was a decent and honest person.

25:1-9

[1] Now Israel remained in Acacia Grove (Shittim), and the people began to commit harlotry with the women of Moab. [2] They invited the people to the sacrifices of their gods, and the

people ate and bowed down to their gods. ³ So Israel was joined to Baal of Peor, and the anger of the LORD was aroused against Israel.

⁴ Then the LORD said to Moses, "Take all the leaders of the people and hang the offenders before the LORD, out in the sun, that the fierce anger of the LORD may turn away from Israel."

⁵ So Moses said to the judges of Israel, "Every one of you kill his men who were joined to Baal of Peor."

⁶ And indeed, one of the children of Israel came and presented to his brethren a Midianite woman in the sight of Moses and in the sight of all the congregation of the children of Israel, who were weeping at the door of the tabernacle of meeting. ⁷ Now when Phinehas the son of Eleazar, the son of Aaron the priest, saw it, he rose from among the congregation and took a javelin in his hand; ⁸ and he went after the man of Israel into the tent and thrust both of them through, the man of Israel, and the woman through her body. So the plague was stopped among the children of Israel. ⁹ And those who died in the plague were twenty-four thousand.

This chapter makes us see to what extent the belief in Moses's teachings had taken root in the Israelites. At the first opportunity, at least some of them forsook his religion in favor of another. But not a man like Moses would relinquish the masterful economic structure he established over time, since the exodus from Egypt; clearly, he must regain control. So he unleashes a plague – one of several he dabbled in not that long ago – and kills twenty-four thousand people, which serves also to satisfy his uncontrollable blood thirst.

28:1-9

¹ Now the LORD spoke to Moses, saying,² "Command the children of Israel, and say to them, 'My offering, My food for My offerings made by fire as a sweet aroma to Me, you shall be careful to offer to Me at their appointed time.'

³ "And you shall say to them, 'This *is* the offering made by fire which you shall offer to the LORD: two male lambs in their

first year without blemish, day by day, as a regular burnt offering.[4] The one lamb you shall offer in the morning, the other lamb you shall offer in the evening,[5] and one-tenth of an ephah of fine flour as a grain offering mixed with one-fourth of a hin of pressed oil. [6] *It is* a regular burnt offering which was ordained at Mount Sinai for a sweet aroma, an offering made by fire to the LORD. [7] And its drink offering *shall be* one-fourth of a hin for each lamb; in a holy *place* you shall pour out the drink to the LORD as an offering. [8] The other lamb you shall offer in the evening; as the morning grain offering and its drink offering, you shall offer *it* as an offering made by fire, a sweet aroma to the LORD.

[9] 'And on the Sabbath day two lambs in their first year, without blemish, and two-tenths *of an ephah* of fine flour as a grain offering, mixed with oil, with its drink offering— [10] *this is* the burnt offering for every Sabbath, besides the regular burnt offering with its drink offering.'"

The fact that after each mass murder Moses goes back to focus on eating delectable food cannot go unnoticed. After God willed certain privileges to Aaron and his offspring for eternity, those fortunate, God-authorized people ask the rest of the community for further 'royalties'. This time, Moses orders two lambs a day, together with his favorite side-dishes. But he goes on to specify that the lambs should be prepared twice daily: one in the morning and one in the evening. The first time I read a similar passage, when the tabernacle of meeting was being built, I wasn't sure if this was indeed the case or whether there was a mistake somewhere. I refer to the lambs that must be prepared on the Sabbath. In this chapter, there is no mistaking the instructions. Apparently, Moses and his entourage preferred eating freshly-prepared food, such that was cooked right before the meal; even on the Sabbath, when you are absolutely forbidden to work nor to light a fire – a law that carries the death penalty for breaking it. Once again, we see that God 'forgets' one of the ten commandments, specifically one the breaking of which is the gravest of offenses:

[8] "Remember the Sabbath day, to keep it holy. [9] Six days you shall labor and do all your work, [10] but the seventh day is the Sabbath of the Lord your God. In it you shall do no work: you, nor your son, nor your daughter, nor your male servant, nor your female servant, nor your cattle, nor your stranger who is within your gates. [11] For in six days the Lord made the heavens and the earth, the sea, and all that is in them, and rested the seventh day. Therefore the Lord blessed the Sabbath day and hallowed it." (Exodus 20:8-17)

This is indeed a very embarrassing situation, seeing as it is God who is ordering all these delicacies for himself.

28:11-15 ... 25

[11] 'At the beginnings of your months you shall present a burnt offering to the LORD: two young bulls, one ram, and seven lambs in their first year, without blemish; [12] three-tenths of an ephah of fine flour as a grain offering, mixed with oil, for each bull; two-tenths of an ephah of fine flour as a grain offering, mixed with oil, for the one ram; [13] and one-tenth of an ephah of fine flour, mixed with oil, as a grain offering for each lamb, as a burnt offering of sweet aroma, an offering made by fire to the LORD. [14] Their drink offering shall be half a hin of wine for a bull, one-third of a hin for a ram, and one-fourth of a hin for a lamb; this is the burnt offering for each month throughout the months of the year. [15] Also one kid of the goats as a sin offering to the LORD shall be offered, besides the regular burnt offering and its drink offering ... [25] And on the seventh day you shall have a holy convocation. You shall do no customary work.'

Moses finds yet another excuse for more sacrifices to God; and please do not forget the fine flour mixed with oil; and of course it wouldn't do to have a meal without wine!

28:26-31

[26] 'Also on the day of the first fruits, when you bring a new grain offering to the LORD at your Feast of Weeks, you shall have a holy convocation. You shall do no customary work. [27] You shall present a burnt offering as a sweet aroma to the LORD: two young bulls, one ram, and seven lambs in their first year, [28] with their grain offering of fine flour mixed with oil: three-tenths of an ephah for each bull, two-tenths for the one ram, [29] and one-tenth for each of the seven lambs; [30] also one kid of the goats, to make atonement for you. [31] Be sure they are without blemish. You shall present them with their drink offerings, besides the regular burnt offering with its grain offering.'

After the battles and the conquests, and the pathological murders, Moses goes back to deal with the business of the favorite dishes for him and his entourage. All these detailed instructions for preparing the food, purportedly according to God's guidelines, only serve to prove that God is a man-made invention.

29:1-6

[1] 'And in the seventh month, on the first day of the month, you shall have a holy convocation. You shall do no customary work. For you it is a day of blowing the trumpets. [2] You shall offer a burnt offering as a sweet aroma to the LORD: one young bull, one ram, and seven lambs in their first year, without blemish. [3] Their grain offering shall be fine flour mixed with oil: three-tenths of an ephah for the bull, two-tenths for the ram, [4] and one-tenth for each of the seven lambs; [5] also one kid of the goats as a sin offering, to make atonement for you; [6] besides the burnt offering with its grain offering for the New Moon, the regular burnt offering with its grain offering, and their drink offerings, according to their ordinance, as a sweet aroma, an offering made by fire to the LORD.'

Increasingly, the god Jehovah gets involved deeper and deeper with procuring food from the people, one could say huge quantities of food, unrelentingly. I don't wish to hurt anyone's feelings, but could it be, might it just be possible, that someone is ordering all this food for himself, and is simply using God's name to mislead the people? No! It couldn't be; because where is God, then? Doesn't he care that the people are being robbed through using His name?

29:7-11

[7] 'On the tenth day of this seventh month you shall have a holy convocation. You shall afflict your souls; you shall not do any work. [8] You shall present a burnt offering to the LORD as a sweet aroma: one young bull, one ram, and seven lambs in their first year. Be sure they are without blemish. [9] Their grain offering shall be of fine flour mixed with oil: three-tenths of an ephah for the bull, two-tenths for the one ram, [10] and one-tenth for each of the seven lambs; [11] also one kid of the goats as a sin offering, besides the sin offering for atonement, the regular burnt offering with its grain offering, and their drink offerings.'

This passage deals with the Day of Atonement. Even on this holy day offerings must be made to God. And why? Because Moses and Aaron reinvented God, and they planned all the holidays and festivals of the Israelite community, including the Day of Atonement; because even on that day they could make the Israelites happily slaughter and burn animals. But only they, Moses and Aaron, knew the truth; so they arranged for themselves, even on the Day of Atonement, sumptuous feasts. Merely recording all this constitutes disdain for human intelligence.

29:12-16

[12] 'On the fifteenth day of the seventh month you shall have a holy convocation. You shall do no customary work, and

you shall keep a feast to the LORD seven days. [13] You shall present a burnt offering, an offering made by fire as a sweet aroma to the LORD: thirteen young bulls, two rams, and fourteen lambs in their first year. They shall be without blemish. [14] Their grain offering shall be of fine flour mixed with oil: three-tenths of an ephah for each of the thirteen bulls, two-tenths for each of the two rams, [15] and one-tenth for each of the fourteen lambs; [16] also one kid of the goats as a sin offering, besides the regular burnt offering, its grain offering, and its drink offering.

29:17-19

[17] 'On the second day present twelve young bulls, two rams, fourteen lambs in their first year without blemish, [18] and their grain offering and their drink offerings for the bulls, for the rams, and for the lambs, by their number, according to the ordinance; [19] also one kid of the goats as a sin offering, besides the regular burnt offering with its grain offering, and their drink offerings.

29:20-26

[20] 'On the third day present eleven bulls, two rams, fourteen lambs in their first year without blemish, [21] and their grain offering and their drink offerings for the bulls, for the rams, and for the lambs, by their number, according to the ordinance; [22] also one goat as a sin offering, besides the regular burnt offering, its grain offering, and its drink offering.

[23] 'On the fourth day present ten bulls, two rams, and fourteen lambs in their first year, without blemish, [24] and their grain offering and their drink offerings for the bulls, for the rams, and for the lambs, by their number, according to the ordinance; [25] also one kid of the goats as a sin offering, besides the regular burnt offering, its grain offering, and its drink offering.

[26] 'On the fifth day present nine bulls, two rams, and fourteen lambs in their first year without blemish,

29:23-25

[23] 'On the fourth day present ten bulls, two rams, and fourteen lambs in their first year, without blemish, [24] and their grain offering and their drink offerings for the bulls, for the rams, and for the lambs, by their number, according to the ordinance; [25] also one kid of the goats as a sin offering, besides the regular burnt offering, its grain offering, and its drink offering.

29:26-28

[26] 'On the fifth day present nine bulls, two rams, and fourteen lambs in their first year without blemish, [27] and their grain offering and their drink offerings for the bulls, for the rams, and for the lambs, by their number, according to the ordinance; [28] also one goat as a sin offering, besides the regular burnt offering, its grain offering, and its drink offering.

29:29-31

[29] 'On the sixth day present eight bulls, two rams, and fourteen lambs in their first year without blemish, [30] and their grain offering and their drink offerings for the bulls, for the rams, and for the lambs, by their number, according to the ordinance; [31] also one goat as a sin offering, besides the regular burnt offering, its grain offering, and its drink offering.

29:32-34

[32] 'On the seventh day present seven bulls, two rams, and fourteen lambs in their first year without blemish, [33] and their grain offering and their drink offerings for the bulls, for the rams, and for the lambs, by their number, according to the ordinance; [34] also one goat as a sin offering, besides the regular burnt offering, its grain offering, and its drink offering.

29:35-40

³⁵ 'On the eighth day you shall have a sacred assembly. You shall do no customary work.³⁶ You shall present a burnt offering, an offering made by fire as a sweet aroma to the LORD: one bull, one ram, seven lambs in their first year without blemish, ³⁷ and their grain offering and their drink offerings for the bull, for the ram, and for the lambs, by their number, according to the ordinance; ³⁸ also one goat as a sin offering, besides the regular burnt offering, its grain offering, and its drink offering.

³⁹ 'These you shall present to the LORD at your appointed feasts (besides your vowed offerings and your freewill offerings) as your burnt offerings and your grain offerings, as your drink offerings and your peace offerings.'"

⁴⁰ So Moses told the children of Israel everything, just as the LORD commanded Moses.

One cannot but notice the huge increase in the amount of meat God orders – via Moses of course – the people to provide. Most of the people were shepherds, and when they left Egypt, they'd been slaves, so it is very likely that most, or even all of them, lacked basic education. But based on what happened to Korah and his company, I believe that in addition to the latter there were others who belonged to the school of non-slaves, who had lived as free men in Egypt, and whom Moses had persuaded to join him in his adventure. However, once in the desert, Moses realized that they can only obstruct him and his methods.

Based on the events, it is easy to deduce that Moses got rid of stragglers, which must have included the sick and the disabled, since he had no way of saving them; he had no hospitals or other means to treat medical problems that cropped up; not to mention that those infirm people slowed down the journey to the 'promised' land. It may sound macabre, but very much in keeping with Moses's behavior. Therefore, it is possible that he took every opportunity he had to get rid of the more educated among the crowd, particularly those who were not under his influence or whom he feared may harm him in some way.

Judging by the huge quantities of cattle and sheep that Moses's parasitical group succeeded in taking away from the shepherds, it's difficult to believe that they gave up the meat of their own free will. But after each of Moses's fits of murder, each taking thousands of lives, and as those attacks and murders persisted and the number of those killed grew, they must have had an effect: the shepherds must have become more submissive and passive, providing the cattle and sheep 'willingly'. Be that as it may, in recent chapters God's function can be summed up as providing food for the ruling elite. There is no way we could have known the details of the murders and the number of people killed, had it not been for Moses's writing everything down, which he didn't fail to do, since this is what God told him to do.

31:1-20

[1] And the LORD spoke to Moses, saying: [2] "Take vengeance on the Midianites for the children of Israel. Afterward you shall be gathered to your people."

[3] So Moses spoke to the people, saying, "Arm some of yourselves for war, and let them go against the Midianites to take vengeance for the LORD on Midian. [4] A thousand from each tribe of all the tribes of Israel you shall send to the war."

[5] So there were recruited from the divisions of Israel one thousand from *each* tribe, twelve thousand armed for war. [6] Then Moses sent them to the war, one thousand from *each* tribe; he sent them to the war with Phinehas the son of Eleazar the priest, with the holy articles and the signal trumpets in his hand. [7] And they warred against the Midianites, just as the LORD commanded Moses, and they killed all the males.[8] They killed the kings of Midian with *the rest of* those who were killed—Evi, Rekem, Zur, Hur and Reba, the five kings of Midian. Balaam the son of Beor they also killed with the sword.

⁹ And the children of Israel took the women of Midian captive, with their little ones, and took as spoil all their cattle, all their flocks, and all their goods. ¹⁰ They also burned with fire all the cities where they dwelt, and all their forts. ¹¹ And they took all the spoil and all the booty—of man and beast.

¹² Then they brought the captives, the booty, and the spoil to Moses, to Eleazar the priest, and to the congregation of the children of Israel, to the camp in the plains of Moab by the Jordan, *across from* Jericho. ¹³ And Moses, Eleazar the priest, and all the leaders of the congregation, went to meet them outside the camp. ¹⁴ But Moses was angry with the officers of the army, *with* the captains over thousands and captains over hundreds, who had come from the battle.

¹⁵ And Moses said to them: "Have you kept all the women alive? ¹⁶ Look, these *women* caused the children of Israel, through the counsel of Balaam, to trespass against the LORD in the incident of Peor, and there was a plague among the congregation of the LORD. ¹⁷ Now therefore, kill every male among the little ones, and kill every woman who has known a man intimately.¹⁸ But keep alive for yourselves all the young girls who have not known a man intimately.¹⁹ And as for you, remain outside the camp seven days; whoever has killed any person, and whoever has touched any slain, purify yourselves and your captives on the third day and on the seventh day. ²⁰ Purify every garment, everything made of leather, everything woven of goats' *hair,* and everything made of wood."

God speaks to Moses and commands him to take revenge of the Midianite before he returns his soul to his creator. This happens out of the blue, without any rhyme or reason. Moses recruits a thousand warriors from each tribe, a total of 12,000 warriors, and sends them under the leadership of Phinehas the son of Eleazar the priest, to kill all Midianite males. This news astounded me. As far as I know, God had assigned to Moses the task of taking out the Canaanites, the Hittites, the Amorites, Perizzite, Girgashite and the Jebusite (Genesis 15:18-21). But God never mentioned Midian. After all, Moses's wife was a Midianite, and Moses had been close to his father-in-law Jethro, who helped him a lot. And so I went searching for any clue that would help me understand why and wherefore. I started by putting together everything that appeared in the Torah about Midian from the creation of the world until this very chapter:

Exodus 2:16-22

[16] Now the priest of Midian had seven daughters. And they came and drew water, and they filled the troughs to water their father's flock. [17] Then the shepherds came and drove them away; but Moses stood up and helped them, and watered their flock.
[18] When they came to Reuel their father, he said, "How is it that you have come so soon today?"
[19] And they said, "An Egyptian delivered us from the hand of the shepherds, and he also drew enough water for us and watered the flock."
[20] So he said to his daughters, "And where is he? Why is it that you have left the man? Call him, that he may eat bread."
[21] Then Moses was content to live with the man, and he gave Zipporah his daughter to Moses. [22] And she bore him a son. He called his name Gershom, for he said, "I have been a stranger in a foreign land."

Exodus 18:1-12

[1] And Jethro, the priest of Midian, Moses's father-in-law, heard of all that God had done for Moses and for Israel His people—that the LORD had brought Israel out of Egypt. [2] Then Jethro, Moses's father-in-law, took Zipporah, Moses's wife, after he had sent her back, [3] with her two sons, of whom the name of one was Gershom (for he said, "I have been a stranger in a foreign land") [4] and the name of the other was Eliezer (for he said, "The God of my father was my help, and delivered me from the sword of Pharaoh"); [5] and Jethro, Moses's father-in-law, came with his sons and his wife to Moses in the wilderness, where he was encamped at the mountain of God. [6]

Now he had said to Moses, "I, your father-in-law Jethro, am coming to you with your wife and her two sons with her."

[7] So Moses went out to meet his father-in-law, bowed down, and kissed him. And they asked each other about their well-being, and they went into the tent. [8] And Moses told his father-in-law all that the LORD had done to Pharaoh and to the Egyptians for Israel's sake, all the hardship that had come upon them on the way, and how the LORD had delivered them. [9] Then Jethro rejoiced for all the good which the LORD had done for Israel, whom He had delivered out of the hand of the Egyptians. [10] And Jethro said, "Blessed be the LORD, who has delivered you out of the hand of the Egyptians and out of the hand of Pharaoh, and who has delivered the people from under the hand of the Egyptians. [11] Now I know that the LORD is greater than all the gods; for in the very thing in which they behaved proudly, He was above them." [12] Then Jethro, Moses's father-in-law, took a burnt offering and other sacrifices to offer to God. And Aaron came with all the elders of Israel to eat bread with Moses's father-in-law before God.

Exodus 18:13-27

[13] And so it was, on the next day, that Moses sat to judge the people; and the people stood before Moses from morning until evening. [14] So when Moses' father-in-law saw all that he did for the people, he said, "What is this thing that you are doing for the people? Why do you alone sit, and all the people stand before you from morning until evening?"

[15] And Moses said to his father-in-law, "Because the people come to me to inquire of God. [16] When they have a difficulty, they come to me, and I judge between one and another; and I make known the statutes of God and His laws."

[17] So Moses's father-in-law said to him, "The thing that you do is not good. [18] Both you and these people who are with you will surely wear yourselves out. For this thing is too much for you; you are not able to perform it by yourself. [19] Listen now to my voice; I will give you counsel, and God will be with you: Stand before God for the people, so that you may bring

the difficulties to God. ²⁰ And you shall teach them the statutes and the laws, and show them the way in which they must walk and the work they must do. ²¹ Moreover you shall select from all the people able men, such as fear God, men of truth, hating covetousness; and place such over them to be rulers of thousands, rulers of hundreds, rulers of fifties, and rulers of tens. ²² And let them judge the people at all times. Then it will be that every great matter they shall bring to you, but every small matter they themselves shall judge. So it will be easier for you, for they will bear the burden with you. ²³ If you do this thing, and God so commands you, then you will be able to endure, and all this people will also go to their place in peace."

²⁴ So Moses heeded the voice of his father-in-law and did all that he had said. ²⁵ And Moses chose able men out of all Israel, and made them heads over the people: rulers of thousands, rulers of hundreds, rulers of fifties, and rulers of tens.²⁶ So they judged the people at all times; the hard cases they brought to Moses, but they judged every small case themselves.

²⁷ Then Moses let his father-in-law depart, and he went his way to his own land.

Numbers 10:29-34

²⁹ Now Moses said to Hobab the son of Reuel the Midianite, Moses's father-in-law, "We are setting out for the place of which the LORD said, 'I will give it to you.' Come with us, and we will treat you well; for the LORD has promised good things to Israel."

³⁰ And he said to him, "I will not go, but I will depart to my own land and to my relatives."

³¹ So Moses said, "Please do not leave, inasmuch as you know how we are to camp in the wilderness, and you can be our eyes. ³² And it shall be, if you go with us—indeed it shall be—that whatever good the LORD will do to us, the same we will do to you."

³³ So they departed from the mountain of the LORD on a journey of three days; and the ark of the covenant of the LORD

went before them for the three days' journey, to search out a resting place for them. [34] And the cloud of the LORD was above them by day when they went out from the camp.

And also: Numbers, chapters 22, 23, 24 – the story of Balaam Ben Beor.

These excerpts about the part Midian played in Moses's life, portrays the following picture: When Moses escaped from Egypt for reasons known best to him alone, he arrived at a well in the Sinai desert, where the locals used to draw water for their flocks. He intervenes on behalf of a group of women in an altercation between the women and men shepherds, and as a result he's invited over to the home of Reuel (a.k.a. Jethro), the priest of Midian. Jethro is honored to have him, and gives him his daughter Zipporah, who bears him two sons. Moses is accepted as part of the family, and becomes Jethro's shepherding partner. Together they roam the desert with Jethro's flock. Until Moses is summoned by God to return to Egypt and deliver the Israelites from bondage. He is to lead them to the promised land, a land of milk and honey, where six other peoples, all God's creatures, are sitting there just waiting to be slaughtered in order to vacate the area for the chosen people.

Later, once Moses and the Israelites are in the desert, Jethro, accompanied by Moses's wife and two kids, comes to greet Moses & Co. Their encounter is affectionate, they bow and hug. Jethro blesses God for having saved Moses from the hands of Pharaoh; he makes a sacrifice to God and invites Aaron and the elders of the community for a feast. Furthermore, the following day, when Jethro witnesses Moses hard at work as a judge, he gives him very sound advice on how to delegate authority. Moses takes his advice, and the method recommended by Jethro is the basis of the method used even today in most countries. At the end of the visit, they bid each other farewell.

The next event concerning Midian is when Moses asks Hobab son of Reuel/Jethro to guide them on their way to the promised land, but the latter declines and prefers to go back home.

Lastly, there's the story of Balaam the Midianite, discussed earlier. Balaam is known throughout Midian as an honest and trustworthy man whose blessings and curses alike result in the desired effects. Therefore Balak king of Moab calls upon him to help him by cursing the Israelites who are besieging him. But Balaam, who is guided by God in all his actions, ends up blessing the Israelites three times, in beautiful Hebrew which leaves in no doubt that it is his native tongue. I must add here that today, thousands of years later, you won't find even ten percent of native Hebrew speakers whose level of command of the language is as high as Balaam's. Balaam put his life on the line on this occasion, but the king of Moab turns out to be an honest and decent fellow, and the two part on friendly terms.

Considering all the above, it is very difficult to understand why Moses recruits an army for one purpose only: to wipe out – purportedly in God's name – the people of Midian, the people to whom his own wife and children belong. It is clear that Balaam Ben Beor was executed simply for being a Midianite. Yet I don't understand why, among all those who were killed, Moses makes a point of naming only Balaam by name (aside from the names of the five Midianite kings.) Judging by the text, it seems to have been a slaughter of a secure people that never saw it coming. There is no mention of a battle or an army coming out to defend its lands. It is doubtful if Midian even had an army. What is clear, however, is that the Midianites were a very rich people: rich in gold, silver, copper, iron, tin and lead; as well as cattle, sheep and donkeys.

Murdering all the men and taking the women captive is a form of brigandage. The entire battle took place during an outbreak of a plague, though neither battle nor plague claimed the life of a single Israelite warrior:

'... [49] and they said to Moses, "Your servants have taken a count of the men of war who *are* under our command, and not a man of us is missing".' (Numbers 31:49)

Therefore I don't think it was a war, but a massacre followed by robbery and plundering. The division of spoils among the participants in the robbery (battle?) also resembles the dividing of loot among bandits.

So what could constitute a serious reason for this event? I believe it is Balaam's presenting himself as God's envoy when he appeared before Balak king of Moab. Apparently, Moses found out about Balaam's presenting himself as God's messenger, and took it as a personal, demeaning offense. Moses, who knew the truth, was offended by the fact that Balaam made use of his invention in showing up before Balak. Even though Balaam did so with honest intentions, since he did indeed believe in the god Jehovah.

Still, there must have been a serious reason for Moses to have acted the way he did. After all the wars and conquests and after dividing the land among the Israelite tribes, Moses understood that there was nothing left for him to do in the new land. He would no longer be able to afford his private army, once all the shepherds with their livestock scattered among the tribes. There would be no more sacrifices and gifts. Moses would no longer be able to collect various taxes in God's name. The time had come to build the new country. People had no choice but to concentrate on the commandment 'Six days you shall labor and do all your work ...' Whoever did not work for a living simply would have nothing to eat, at least until a new way was invented to make an honest living.

But most important of all: Moses and his men had cold-bloodedly murdered more than a hundred thousand innocent people. According to local customs, if a person was murdered, for whatever reason, his family must avenge his death – an eye for an eye, a tooth for a tooth. Moses knew full well that he would not be able to survive among the hundreds of thousands of relatives of the slain men. He therefore had to retire, but needed to quickly pull off one last job before disappearing with a fortune. Knowing that Midian has no army to speak of, it would be easy to take them out and rob them of their riches. Moses recruits his army from among the men who'd helped him in previous murderous events, naturally naming God as the organizer of the murder and plunder. It could be that Moses had some of these associates – who today would be treated as war criminals -- join him in his retirement. Together, each with his share of the loot, they go back to the desert, where they start over. Of course, this group disappeared along with Moses without leaving a trace. And since Moses was the only one who recorded his history and that of the Israelites, it is quite possible that he continued writing down his own story and that of his cohorts after they parted ways from the rest of the Israelite community.

For all we know, these writings might still be discovered, one of this days, hidden in a one of the caves in the Sinai peninsula.

Epilogue

Genesis 11:31

[31] And Terah took his son Abram and his grandson Lot, the son of Haran, and his daughter-in-law Sarai, his son Abram's wife, and they went out with them from Ur of the Chaldeans to go to the land of Canaan; and they came to Haran and dwelt there.

Abram's family – whose name would later be changed by Jehovah to Abraham – decides to emigrate from Ur Kaśdim (Ur of the Chaldees), to the land of Canaan. Abraham's life is full of various adventures during which the existence of the god Jehovah is revealed to him, and only to him and not to any other living soul to this very day.

Based on several events in Abraham's life I was able to conclude that Abraham suffered from hallucinations and tricks of the imagination, the most notable of which are the binding of Isaac, and the anxiety attacks he had occasionally, when he feared that kings desired his wife Sarah and wanted to murder him and take her away from him. This could be perfectly rational and accepted thinking, were it not for the fact that the last time Abraham had these thoughts, his wife was already ninety years old.

Abraham's lineage continues with his son Isaac, with whom faith didn't stick, then continues with his grandson Jacob, who was a scoundrel already at a young age: First he bought his elder brother's birthright for the price of a bowl of lentil stew, then he continued to deceive his father into blessing him instead of his brother Esau. Having pulled off that trick, he fled, and even when he decided to come back home to the land of Canaan, he did so with trepidation, fearing that Esau would take revenge on him for his earlier misdoings.

This in fact is the starting point of the mantra 'The God of Abraham, Isaac and Jacob', which continues to appear, compounded by various promises by Jehovah of giving land, land that was at the time populated by other peoples who, according to that theory, were also beings created by the same god, Jehovah. Then starts a dark period for this people, until the advent of Moses.

Somehow it came to pass that the entire Israelite people is trapped in the kingdom of Egypt, living there and doing hard labor as slaves, and under strict restrictions as to the permitted birth-rate. Until the day when Pharaoh, the ruler of Egypt, decreed that all Hebrew male newborns were to be thrown into the Nile. And so baby Moses, too, is thrown into the Nile. But in his case, this done in a most elegant way: he is placed in a well-padded bullrushes basket while his sister Miriam keeps an eye on him from her spot along the river bank. Luckily for him, the basket is picked up by Pharaoh's daughter who came down to the river to bathe. Consequently, Moses lives like a prince in the bosom of the Egyptian royal family, receiving the best education available at the time in the world.

However, at this point Moses undergoes a crisis about which no satisfactory explanation is given in the book of Exodus. As a result, he is forced to leave everything behind and escape towards the Sinai desert. It would seem that he had a serious falling-out with Pharaoh, king of Egypt; perhaps Pharaoh considered Moses's behavior to be a mark of disrespect, or a blot on his honor, considering that Moses came from a people of shepherds, who were considered the lowest of the low in Egypt; not to mention his being born to a nation of slaves. Whatever the case may be, something unforgivable had taken place, and Moses had to leave. In the desert, Moses meets Jethro and is accepted as one of the family. Jethro lets him become one of his shepherds, and together they herd their sheep through the Sinai desert, criss-crossing it in all directions according to the weather and the location of the best grazing grounds. And so Moses becomes familiar with the desert and its aspects through the seasons, all year round.

I suspect that ever since his fleeing Egypt, revenge simmered within Moses. Perhaps already when he first saw the phenomenon of high and low tide on the Nile, the seeds of a revenge plan started taking shape in his mind. Moses decides to bring Pharaoh to the spot where the tide is the strongest, on a certain date of which he was aware from his earlier observations. Moses must have been a very confident and charismatic person to pull it off. He picks up and, leaving everything behind, including wife and kids, sets out on his own for Egypt, heading for an adventure whose outcome is unknown…

Once Moses arrives in Egypt, he thinks of his family there, contacts them, and meets up with Aaron, his elder brother, taking him into his confidence and telling him of his plans. The main problem is, how to bring Pharaoh to the tide spot. That's probably when they come up with the idea of causing all the slaves to flee and concentrate at that spot, which would cause Pharaoh and his men to follow them. Aaron was the one who thought up the idea of dressing up this idea in a religious guise, probably because he already had information about messianic stirrings among the slaves – something that is bound to happen sooner or later wherever there are oppressed people. Aaron tells Moses about the mantra "the God of Abraham, Isaac and Jacob", and Moses picks it up, adding himself as next in line: he himself will appear as the messenger of the god Jehovah, who has come to free the oppressed and lead them to the Promised Land.

All this planning required very accurate timing. Moses, who was a highly educated man, planned the operation with mathematical precision. First of all, Moses teaches his brother magic tricks that he learnt from Egypt's best magicians, in order to impress a delegation of the slaves and persuade them to organize Operation Escape. The performance is highly successful, and thus Moses is 'elected'" to represent the people as the messenger of the god Jehovah. According to Moses's time table, there was still enough time left until the tide goes out, so Moses channels all his energies into giving Pharaoh a very hard time, all the more so since he, Moses, is really enjoying himself. That's why he resorted to the ten plagues, when the last one in itself would have been enough to send Pharaoh and his troops in hot pursuit of Moses. Moses is wary, though, afraid that this Pharaoh might recognize his voice; after all, Moses was one of the household for many years. Therefore he takes precautions by pretending to have a stammer, and only once he's safely in the desert does the stammer disappear.

And so time passes and the big day arrives:

Exodus 14:1-14

[14] Now the Lord spoke to Moses, saying: [2] "Speak to the children of Israel, that they turn and camp before Pi Hahiroth, between Migdol and the sea, opposite Baal Zephon; you shall camp before it by the sea. [3] For Pharaoh will say of the children of Israel, 'They are bewildered by the land; the wilderness has closed them in.' [4] Then I will harden Pharaoh's heart, so that he will pursue them; and I will gain honor over Pharaoh and over all his army, that the Egyptians may know that I am the Lord." And they did so.

[5] Now it was told to the king of Egypt that the people had fled, and the heart of Pharaoh and his servants was turned against the people; and they said, "Why have we done this, that we have let Israel go from serving us?" [6] So he made ready his chariot and took his people with him. [7] Also, he took six hundred choice chariots, and all the chariots of Egypt with captains over every one of them. [8] And the Lord hardened the heart of Pharaoh king of Egypt, and he pursued the children of Israel; and the children of Israel went out with boldness. [9] So the Egyptians pursued them, all the horses and chariots of Pharaoh, his horsemen and his army, and overtook them camping by the sea beside Pi Hahiroth, before Baal Zephon.

[10] And when Pharaoh drew near, the children of Israel lifted their eyes, and behold, the Egyptians marched after them. So they were very afraid, and the children of Israel cried out to the Lord. [11] Then they said to Moses, "Because there were no graves in Egypt, have you taken us away to die in the wilderness? Why have you so dealt with us, to bring us up out of Egypt? [12] Is this not the word that we told you in Egypt, saying, 'Let us alone that we may serve the Egyptians'? For it

would have been better for us to serve the Egyptians than that we should die in the wilderness."

[13] And Moses said to the people, "Do not be afraid. Stand still, and see the salvation of the Lord, which He will accomplish for you today. For the Egyptians whom you see today, you shall see again no more forever. [14] The Lord will fight for you, and you shall hold your peace."

Moses, who is on top of things and knows everything that's about to happen, makes the most of the situation and calms the people down, to show them that he and Jehovah are fully coordinated:

Exodus 14:15-17

[15] And the LORD said to Moses, "Why do you cry to Me? Tell the children of Israel to go forward. [16] But lift up your rod, and stretch out your hand over the sea and divide it. And the children of Israel shall go on dry ground through the midst of the sea. [17] And I indeed will harden the hearts of the Egyptians, and they shall follow them. So I will gain honor over Pharaoh and over all his army, his chariots, and his horsemen."

I don't quite understand why Jehovah would be so eager to earn the Egyptians' respect, knowing full well as he did that they're on their way to drown in the Nile. Also, it's important to keep in mind that it was Jehovah who created the Egyptian people in the first place.

It was no mean feat, organizing and leading some million people to the brink of the low tide that was about to take place at a specific point and time, but Moses kept to his schedule and the operation was a resounding success. Following that success, Moses began leading his people in the direction of Mount Sinai, which was known at the time to be a sacred place for many desert tribes. That's where Moses decided to give Jehovah a new form, and perhaps even step into Jehovah's shoes and declare himself a god. Prior to that, Moses carried out a host of ceremonies designed to aggrandize Jehovah, and finally decided to remain Jehovah's sole messenger on earth, which is a pretty respectable position.

Moses worked hard to make the people believe in Jehovah, and did indeed lead the people according to the mantra which his brother Aaron taught him. Moses was very knowledgeable about the various tribes populating the land of Canaan, first from his studies in Egypt, and later from everything he picked up during his wanderings in the desert with Jethro. He therefore led his people to all the locations he was already familiar with, and took advantage of every opportunity he had to impress his people and implant in them the belief in Jehovah, always presenting himself as Jehovah's messenger. Though Moses had no military background, he was determined to be true to his word and lead the people to the Promised Land. He therefore initiates a military conflict with the Amalekites, only to find out that the Israelites are not ready to go to war over his promises, for the sake of '…every man under his vine and under his fig-tree' but would rather go back to Egypt to live there as slaves.

Early on, Moses organizes a private army for himself, comprising, as it turns out, members of the tribe of Levi. Also early on, Moses 'publishes a book of laws, the essence of which is the ten most important commandments, aimed at making it possible for such a large concentration of people journeying together to live in a relatively orderly fashion. And so Moses continues to add new laws and rules, with the punishment for breaking them being sacrifices to Jehovah, a form of proffering food to Jehovah. This food, obviously, supplied sustenance to Moses's private army and all his entourage – the persons close to him and their families. Obviously, this led to the creation of an increasingly wide stratum of social parasites around Moses. Also early on, Moses succeeded in getting most of the gold out of the hands of the people. Originally, he did so by requesting contributions for the building of the Tabernacle (also known as "the Tent of Meeting"); the rest of their gold he elicited through a provocation he initiated in collaboration with his brother Aaron, when the latter built the golden calf. Anyone who got in his way and interfered with his actions he simply destroyed. If we consider this journey through the desert, there is no mention of sick or injured people, and how they were treated. Those were promptly gotten rid of by Moses, together with anyone who dared complain about him or about Jehovah, always working under Jehovah's orders, prefaced with the words '…and the LORD spoke unto Moses, saying…'

Moses is shown to be a most ruthless killer who, according to my estimates, based only on the words of the Bible, killed – aided by his private army and lackeys – more than seventy thousand people, and innocent ones at that. He habitually kept a record of the number of victims immediately after the killings, supposedly as he was instructed by Jehovah. To those numbers we can add the slaying of the *Midianites* who were murdered and plundered for no good reason and despite being friends to the Israelites and believers in Jehovah. Moses does not neglect to mention in his book that, during the killing and the looting, not one of the Israelites was killed. This massacre, too, Moses puts down as a special request from Jehovah, to be carried out before he, Moses, returns his soul to his creator.

The murder of the Midianite people seems very odd to me: Based on the blessing that Balaam bestowed on the Israelites, it seems that their language was Hebrew; and based on the meetings between Jehovah and Balaam in the affair of Balak king of Moab, it seems that they, too, believed in Jehovah. Is it possible that the reason for this genocide was Moses's hatred for his father-in-law Jethro? Or because Jethro brought Moses's wife and kids to him in the desert? Or perhaps as revenge because Hovav, Jethro's son, didn't want to be Moses's guide, replacing Jehovah's column of smoke by day and column of fire by night? Another possibility is that Moses heard of Balaam's meetings with Jehovah, and got very angry that Balaam was using his own methods in his contacts with Jehovah for his meetings with Balak king of Moab.

In conclusion, I can say I found the truth to be written in the books of the Torah, and it is not true that anyone can interpret the written words as they see fit, unless they are liars and charlatans. A point that reinforces the truth of what is written is the story of Moses and Hobab: Moses asks Hobab, son of Reuel, to serve as guide and show him the way to the Promised Land. Moses even tries to bribe Hobab son of Reuel by promising him that, when Moses is given the Promised Land by Jehovah, part of it will go to him, i.e. to Reuel. The surprising thing here is that Moses apparently was not willing to rely solely on the pillar of smoke by day and the pillar of fire by night, although these were supposed to be manifestations of Jehovah himself leading the camp. And Moses even had no compunctions about writing this down in the relevant chapter (Numbers 10:29-34).

Finally, I can say that all faiths and religions, of which there are thousands, are chiefly businesses based on high income; some religions are businesses with a turnover of billions. And for those who fear lest some religions might disappear, I can reassure him that in the future more religions are bound to pop up, all equipped with some savior or antoher.

It is very difficult to understand man's way of thinking. Take, for example, the issue of tobacco smoking. In the early 1950s, research showed beyond any doubt that smoking causes lung cancer. Since then science has found that practically all diseases are somehow linked to smoking, and smoking harms even non-smokers who are simply in proximity to the smoker; most smokers die of smoking and its various complications, not counting those who die in wars and traffic accidents. Despite that, the number of smokers keeps growing, even as new knowledge about additional smoking-related diseases comes to light. Add to that people using various hallucinogenic drugs; their numbers are growing every day, despite the fact that, of their free will, they are destroying their bodies and their health, turning into a wreck. And this may be the place to also mention noise, which is known to be highly damaging to man. Some scientists think that it is specifically man-made noise that will eventually wipe out humanity from the face of the earth. Despite all that, musical instruments are manufactured today that increase the noise several times over, compared to similar instruments made in the past. Currently, it's nearly impossible to enter a functions hall without encountering a deafening noise produced by those 'musical instruments'. And what about pollution that is destroying our planet?

I'd like to end on a humorous note:

One day a man of about thirty with a black beard and long curly sideburns knocked at my door and tried to sell me some Kabbalah books that he carried in a big backpack.
- Listen here, I'll buy from you any book you like from the collection in your bag, on one condition.
- What condition?
- Take out any book, open it at whatever page you like, start reading at whatever line you wish, and if you can explain to me what it says, I'll buy the book.
The man took out a book, opened it in the middle, and together we began reading one sentence after another which he chose. Naturally, neither of us understood what it said. The man was somewhat taken aback, and took out a different book from his satchel, then another and another, opened them at various places and read entire sentences, but in none of it made any sense.
- Listen, I said to him, how can it be that these books are written in Hebrew, we both speak the language, and yet no sentence is clear to us?
The man replied:
- Do you know who I am?
- No.
- I'm God!
I exploded in a series of curses in five languages which I'd rather not put in writing.
- Why are you cursing me like that?
- You don't know why?
- No, I don't know why.
To which I replied in a very loud voice, attempting to imitate the voice of God:
- Because I am God!

At which he smiled broadly, stretched out his hand warmly, saying,
- Kudos, my friend.
And so we parted amicably.